meet *Emilie Richards*

Photo by Creation Waits

*N*ow a USA TODAY bestselling author of women's fiction, Emilie Richards recalls fondly the months she served as a VISTA volunteer in the Arkansas Ozarks.

"This was the country's third poorest county," Emilie said in an interview from her Virginia home. "They had no phones, no safe water supply and no indoor plumbing. But the women created beauty out of nothing—turning scraps of old clothing and feedsacks into exquisitely beautiful quilts."

Emilie said the women insisted she quilt with them in the evenings, "and then later, they'd take out my stitches," she laughingly recalls of her early attempts at the craft.

The 20-year-old college student was left with a richness of experience and a love of quilting that would forever change her life and ultimately inspire a series of novels about the age-old craft. Emilie went on to finish her undergraduate degree in American studies and her master's in family development. She served as a therapist in a mental health center, as a parent services coordinator for Head Start families and in several pastoral counseling centers. Now a full-time writer, Emilie has drawn on these experiences while crafting more than 50 novels.

In *Touching Stars*, Emilie's fourth and newest Shenandoah Album novel in the popular series, quilts form a colorful backdrop in a gracious bed-and-breakfast. The owner of the inn is a hardworking single mother who learns from a Civil War widow the importance of recognizing love while letting go of the past. Four pattern books, *Quilt Along with Emilie Richards*—*Wedding Ring, Endless Chain, Lover's Knot,* and *Touching Stars*—offer fans a chance to create their own versions of the quilts in her novels.

To learn more about Emilie, visit her Web site at www.emilierichards.com.

LEISURE ARTS, INC.
Little Rock, Arkansas

Read the books that *Inspired* the projects

Leisure Arts is pleased to offer these quilting instruction books as companions to Emilie's compelling Shenandoah Album stories. Each *Quilt Along with Emilie Richards* pattern book includes instructions to create quilts that are featured in the novels. The latest is *Quilt Along with Emilie Richards: Touching Stars*, offering 9 projects as made by the SCC quilters and Miranda Duncan, or like those displayed in the Daughter of the Stars bed-and-breakfast. These include designs for bed quilts, wall hangings, a table runner, pot holder, and pillow.

Enhanced with excerpts from the novels, each *Quilt Along with Emilie Richards* book gives the reader a glimpse of the unforgettable characters created by the gifted author.

Now there are four exciting novels in Emilie Richards' *Shenandoah Album* Series, *Wedding Ring*, *Endless Chain*, *Lover's Knot*, and *Touching Stars*. Each is rich with family drama, romance — and quilts!

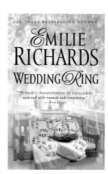 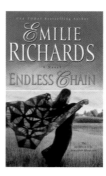 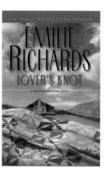 

Read Emilie Richards' *Shenandoah Album* novels, then quilt along with the good folks of Toms Brook and Fitch Crossing Road. You may just discover a lifelong passion of your very own!

Meet the characters from *Touching Stars*

gayle fortman

Gayle Fortman has built a good life for herself and her three sons in the Shenandoah Valley of Virginia. Divorced from charismatic broadcast journalist Eric Fortman, Gayle has made a success of Daughter of the Stars, a popular bed-and-breakfast that she has lovingly decorated with star-themed quilts. She has even maintained a cordial relationship with Eric, covering with the boys for his absences and broken promises. Luckily, Travis Allen, her closest neighbor and best friend, has been a loving surrogate father to the boys. But now, on the eve of oldest son Jared's graduation, Eric returns. Realizing this might be the last chance for her sons to establish a bond with their father, Gayle offers Eric a summer at the inn to put things right. But can the pieces of their broken lives be mended, or are they better laid to rest?

"The inn's Lone Star room was one of Gayle's favorites. Each of the eight bedrooms was named after a different star quilt and decorated in harmony with the colors of the quilt displayed there. The Lone Star room was dominated by an Amish made Lone Star wall hanging in southwestern sunset colors. The fact that Eric had been born in the Lone Star state gave the decision to house him here the necessary note of humor—and they were going to need all the laughter they could muster."

—from Touching Stars

"Maybe Eric's marriage to Gayle could have worked if he had been someone else, someone better. Eric rarely beat himself up. But he had come to the realization that he rarely put anyone else's needs ahead of his own. Three days when he had believed each breath might be his last had firmed up that conclusion. And in the weeks since he'd been held hostage, he'd had time to consider everything about his life. Once he was out of danger, Eric had slammed up against a wall of anger so thick, so tall, that he wasn't sure he could ever scale it to see what was on the other side."

—from Touching Stars

eric fortman

Eric nearly lost his life in Afghanistan. Worse, he has lost his way and his courage, and needs a place to recover. When Gayle offers him a home for the summer, he finds that he can't refuse. But after so many years of being an absentee father, he doesn't know how to repair his relationship with his sons. The two oldest boys resent him, while the youngest is confused by Eric's rejection. And then there's Gayle herself—his ex-wife's nurturing ways are a balm to Eric's wounded spirit, tempting him to reconsider a relationship that was rocky at the best of times. With so many challenges to face at home, Eric may decide there's more peace to be found in the war-torn hills of Afghanistan than in the beautiful Shenandoah Valley.

helen henry

The most celebrated quilter in Shenandoah County is Helen Henry, a pragmatic, elderly woman who believes she can teach anyone to make quilts, including Gayle Fortman and Gayle's middle son, Noah. When Gayle asks the Shenandoah Community Church Bee quilters to make a quilt at her bed-and-breakfast, Helen sees a chance to recruit more quilters for the Bee. It's also a fine opportunity for her to share some local history with anyone who cares to sit at the quilting frame. And by Helen's reckoning, Gayle should know a little something about a mysterious quilter named Miranda Duncan who lived on Gayle's property long ago.

"'I got another story to tell,' Helen took tiny, perfectly spaced stitches as she spoke. 'About the woman who lived in that farmhouse used to be across the way. She was a young woman when the Civil War began. She lived in that house alone until the day she died. I think she was close to a hundred. By the time she got to be old, the house was too big for one person to care for. It started to show its age. And old houses, purt near abandoned like that, they get a reputation, if you know what I mean.'"

—from Touching Stars

5

Touching Stars Quilt

Piecing perfect diamond shapes used to be a goal achieved only by experienced quilters, but rotary cutting increases accuracy while speeding up the whole process—a bonus that all modern quilters can enjoy.

Finished Quilt Size: 59¹/₂" x 59¹/₂" (151 cm x 151 cm)

CUTTING OUT THE PIECES

Follow Rotary Cutting, page 50, to cut fabric. All strips are cut across the width of the fabric unless otherwise noted. Outer borders include an extra 4" of length for "insurance" and will be trimmed after assembling quilt top center. All measurements include $^1/_4$" seam allowances.

From brown print fabric:
- Cut 4 strips $7^5/_8$"w. From these strips, cut 16 **background squares** $7^5/_8$" x $7^5/_8$".
- Cut 2 *lengthwise* **top/bottom outer borders** $4^1/_2$" x $63^1/_4$".
- Cut 2 *lengthwise* **side outer borders** $4^1/_2$" x $55^1/_4$".

From remaining width:
- Cut 4 squares $11^1/_4$" x $11^1/_4$". Cut squares twice diagonally to make 16 **background triangles**.

From red print fabric:
- Cut 12 strips $1^3/_4$"w. Cut each strip in half (at fold) to make 24 **long strips**.

From *each* green and blue print fabric:
- Cut 12 strips $1^3/_4$"w. Cut each strip in half (at fold) to make 24 **long strips**.
- Cut 2 **short strips** $1^3/_4$" x 14".

From gold print fabric:
- Cut 12 strips $1^3/_4$"w. Cut each strip in half (at fold) to make 24 **long strips**.
- Cut 1 square $3^3/_4$" x $3^3/_4$". Cut square *twice* diagonally to make 4 **border triangles**.

YARDAGE REQUIREMENTS

Yardage is based on 43"/44" (109 cm/112 cm) wide fabric.

$2^7/_8$ yds (2.6 m) of brown print fabric

$^3/_4$ yd (69 cm) *each* of red print, green print, and blue print fabrics

$^7/_8$ yd (80 cm) of gold print fabric

$3^7/_8$ yds (3.5 m) of fabric for backing

$^7/_8$ yd (80 cm) of fabric for binding

You will also need:
68" x 68" (173 cm x 173 cm) piece of batting

6" x 24" acrylic ruler with a 45° angle marking

"The top the quilters had created—after their usual good-natured squabbling—was perfect for the inn's stairwell. Using Civil War reproduction fabrics of reds and golds, blues and greens, they had designed and beautifully executed a stunning wall hanging of four traditional stars, the arms of each touching those of its neighbors. The pattern was known as Touching Stars."

—from Touching Stars

7

Strip Set A
(make 7)

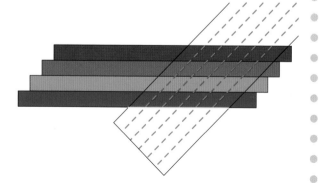

Strip Set B
(make 5)

Strip Set C
(make 5)

Strip Set D
(make 5)

Strip Set E
(make 1)

Fig. 1

MAKING THE UNITS

Follow **Piecing***, page 51, and* **Pressing***, page 54. Use* $^1/_4$*" seam allowances throughout.*

1. Sew 4 **long strips** together lengthwise in color order shown, offsetting strips by 1" to make **Strip Set A**. Make 7 **Strip Set A's** and 5 *each* of **Strip Sets B**, **C**, and **D**.

2. Sew 2 **short strips** together lengthwise in color order shown, offsetting strips by 1" to make **Strip Set E**.

3. Place 1 **Strip Set A** on cutting mat with blue strip on top. Aligning 45° line on ruler (shown in yellow) with bottom edge of **Strip Set A** (**Fig. 1**), trim right edge.

4. Rotate **Strip Set A** so that trimmed edge is on left and red strip is on top. Aligning 45° line on ruler with bottom edge of **Strip Set A**, place ruler on **Strip Set A** so that the 1³/₄" mark on ruler is aligned with trimmed edge (**Fig. 2**). Cut on right side of ruler to make **Unit 1**. Moving ruler to right, aligning 1³/₄" mark with cut edge, and cutting on right side of ruler, continue making **Unit 1's**. Repeat with remaining **Strip Set A's** to make a *total* of 44 **Unit 1's**.

5. From **Strip Set B's**, cut 32 **Unit 2's**.

6. From **Strip Set C's**, cut 32 **Unit 3's**.

7. From **Strip Set D's**, cut 32 **Unit 4's**.

8. From **Strip Set E**, cut 4 **Unit 5's**.

9. Sew 4 **long strips** together lengthwise in color order shown, offsetting strips by 1" to make **Strip Set F**. Make 2 **Strip Sets F's**.

10. Sew 2 **short strips** together lengthwise in color order shown, offsetting strips by 1" to make **Strip Set G**.

"*Gayle enlisted her middle son, Noah, to help rearrange furniture in the morning room so the quilters could set up the old-fashioned quilt frame that would take up the center of the room. If they desired, guests of the inn would be encouraged to quilt a few stitches. By summer's end, the Touching Stars quilt would be finished, bound, and hung.*"
—from Touching Stars

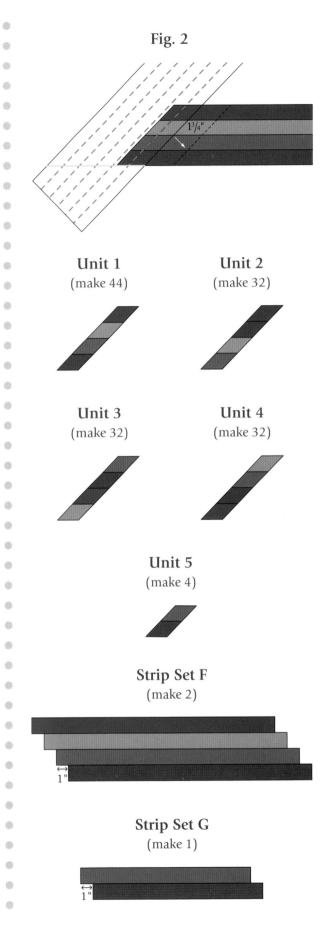

Fig. 2

Unit 1
(make 44)

Unit 2
(make 32)

Unit 3
(make 32)

Unit 4
(make 32)

Unit 5
(make 4)

Strip Set F
(make 2)

Strip Set G
(make 1)

9

Fig. 3

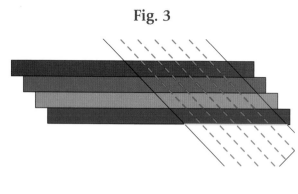

Fig. 4

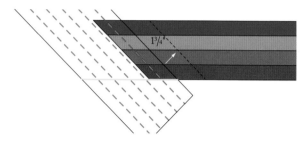

Unit 6
(make 12)

Unit 7
(make 4)

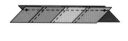

Fig. 5

$^1/_4$" $^1/_4$"

Fig. 6

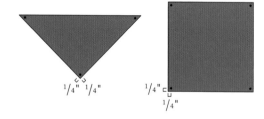

$^1/_4$" $^1/_4$" $^1/_4$"
                        $^1/_4$"

Fig. 7

Diamond Unit
(make 32)

11. Place 1 **Strip Set F** on cutting mat with blue strip on top. Aligning 45° line on ruler (shown in yellow) with bottom edge of **Strip Set F** (**Fig. 3**), trim right edge.

12. Rotate **Strip Set F** so that trimmed edge is on left and red strip is on top. Aligning 45° line on ruler with bottom edge of **Strip Set F**, place ruler on **Strip Set F** so that the $1^3/_4$" mark on ruler is aligned with trimmed edge (**Fig. 4**). Cut on right side of ruler to make **Unit 6**. Moving ruler to right, aligning $1^3/_4$" mark with cut edge, and cutting on right side of ruler, continue making **Unit 6's**. Repeat with remaining **Strip Set F** to make a *total* of 12 **Unit 6's**.

13. From **Strip Set G**, cut 4 **Unit 7's**.

MARKING THE $^1/_4$" SEAM ALLOWANCES

Because of the diamond shapes, marking seam allowances at corners of Units and background pieces will allow for more accurate piecing.

1. On wrong side of each **Unit 1 – 7**, make a dot with pencil $^1/_4$" from edges in each corner (**Fig. 5**).

2. On wrong side of each **background square** and **triangle**, mark a dot with pencil $^1/_4$" from edges in each corner (**Fig 6**).

MAKING THE DIAMOND UNITS

1. Sew 1 each of **Units 1 – 4** together in order shown to make **Diamond Unit**. (*Note: When making Diamond Units, refer to Fig. 7 and match dots and long edges of Units.*) Make 32 **Diamond Units**.

ASSEMBLING THE QUILT TOP CENTER

*Follow **Working with In-Set Seams**, page 53, to assemble quilt top center. Refer to **Quilt Top Diagram**, page 12, for placement.*

1. Sew 2 **Diamond Units** together to make **Unit 8**. Make 16 **Unit 8's**.

2. Sew 4 **Unit 8's** together to make **Star**. Make 4 **Stars**.

3. Sew 4 **background triangles** and then 4 **background squares** to 1 **Star** to make **Star Unit**. Make 4 **Star Units**.

4. Sew 4 **Star Units** together to complete quilt top center.

MAKING THE INNER BORDER

1. Sew 3 **Unit 1's** together to make **Unit 9**. Make 4 **Unit 9's**.

2. Sew 3 **Unit 6's** together to make **Unit 10**. Make 4 **Unit 10's**.

3. Sew 1 **Unit 5**, 1 **Unit 7**, and 1 **border triangle** together to make **Unit 11**. Make 4 **Unit 11's**.

4. Referring to **Quilt Top Diagram**, page 12, sew 1 **Unit 9**, 1 **Unit 10**, and 1 **Unit 11** together to make **inner border**. Make 4 **inner borders**.

ADDING THE BORDERS

1. With right sides together and matching centers and corners, pin **top inner border** to quilt top. Sew **top inner border** to quilt top, beginning and ending exactly ¹/₄" from each corner of quilt top. Backstitch at beginning and ending of stitching to reinforce.

2. Repeat Step 1 to sew **bottom** and then **side inner borders** to quilt top.

3. With right sides together and matching edges, fold 1 corner of quilt top diagonally as shown in **Fig. 8**. Sew ends of borders together (shown in pink). Repeat for other corners.

4. To determine length of **side outer borders**, measure *length* of quilt top. Trim **side outer borders** to determined length. Matching centers and corners, sew **side outer borders** to quilt top.

5. To determine length of **top/bottom outer borders**, measure *width* of quilt top (including added borders). Trim **top/bottom outer borders** to determined length. Matching centers and corners, sew **top/bottom outer borders** to quilt top.

Unit 8
(make 16)

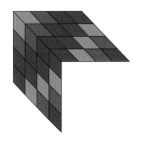

Star
(make 4)

Unit 9
(make 4)

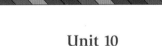

Unit 10
(make 4)

Unit 11
(make 4)

Fig. 8

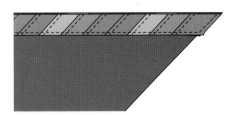

11

COMPLETING THE QUILT

1. Follow **Quilting**, page 55, to mark, layer, and quilt as desired. Our quilt is machine quilted in the ditch on outer edges of stars and inner border. A curved outline is quilted in each diamond piece of the stars. A large "V" is quilted in each outer setting triangle. Feather patterns are quilted in remaining setting pieces and outer border.

2. Follow **Making a Hanging Sleeve**, page 59, if a hanging sleeve is desired.

3. Cut a 25" square of binding fabric. Follow **Binding**, page 60, to bind quilt using 2¹/₈"w bias binding with mitered corners.

Quilt Top Diagram

"*On Tuesday the quilters put the final touches in the breathtaking Touching Stars quilt. Helen insisted that Noah and Eric be there to help the women remove it from the frame. And when the quilt was off, she turned it over and told both of them to sign their names on the label alongside the names of all the members of the SCC Bee.*"

—from Touching Stars

Virginia Star Quilt

This design is sometimes called "Easy Virginia Star" because it is comprised of fewer pieces than other quilts of the same name. The Virginia Star quilt that Miranda Duncan stitched was made of shirting scraps. In nineteenth century America, butternut husks were often used to dye fabrics.

Finished Quilt Size: 44³/₄" x 44³/₄" (114 cm x 114 cm)
Finished Block Size: 12" x 12" (30 cm x 30 cm)

CUTTING OUT THE PIECES

Follow **Rotary Cutting**, page 50, to cut fabric. Borders are cut longer than needed and will be trimmed after assembling quilt top center. All measurements include $^1/_4$" seam allowances.

From cream print fabric for inner border:
- Cut 4 *lengthwise* **inner borders** $1^1/_2$" x $48^1/_2$".

From tan print fabric for outer border:
- Cut 4 *lengthwise* **outer borders** $3^1/_2$" x $48^1/_2$".

YARDAGE REQUIREMENTS

Yardage is based on 43"/44" (109 cm/112 cm) wide fabric.

$2^1/_8$ yds (1.9 m) of cream print fabric (includes inner border)

$2^1/_4$ yds (2.1 m) of tan print fabric (includes outer border)

$^7/_8$ yd (80 cm) of green print fabric

$^7/_8$ yd (80 cm) of purple print fabric

3 yds (2.7 m) of fabric for backing

$^3/_4$ yd (69 cm) of fabric for binding

You will also need: 53" x 53" (135 cm x 135 cm) piece of batting

"'When Ma had time in the evenings, she would quilt a row or two. This quilt was one she called Virginia Star. She had never told me as much, but before the quilt was stretched out on the frame, I noticed cloth from shirts she had made for my father and some that was dyed the same butternut hue as his uniform.'"

—Robby Duncan, Touching Stars

Unit 1
(make 20)

Unit 2
(make 20)

Unit 3
(make 20)

Unit 4
(make 20)

Unit 5
(make 20)

Unit 6
(make 20)

Unit 7
(make 20)

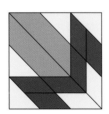

Block A
(make 5)

PAPER PIECING THE BLOCKS

Photocopy 36 copies each of Paper Piecing Foundation A – D patterns, page 19. Follow Paper Piecing, page 53, to paper piece Blocks.

1. Use 1 foundation A and tan print for area 1, purple print for area 2, and cream print for area 3 to make **Unit 1**. Make 20 **Unit 1's**.

2. Use 1 foundation B and tan print for area 1, purple print for area 2, and cream print for area 3 to make **Unit 2**. Make 20 **Unit 2's**.

3. Use 1 foundation C and green print for area 1, purple print for area 2, and cream print for areas 3 and 4 to make **Unit 3**. Make 20 **Unit 3's**.

4. Use 1 foundation D and green print for area 1, purple print for area 2, and cream print for areas 3 and 4 to make **Unit 4**. Make 20 **Unit 4's**.

5. Sew 1 **Unit 1** and 1 **Unit 3** together to make **Unit 5**. Make 20 **Unit 5's**.

6. Sew 1 **Unit 2** and 1 **Unit 4** together to make **Unit 6**. Make 20 **Unit 6's**.

7. Sew 1 **Unit 5** and 1 **Unit 6** together to make **Unit 7**. Make 20 **Unit 7's**.

8. Sew 4 **Unit 7's** together to make **Block A**. Make 5 **Block A's**.

"'Strange men, some in tattered butternut or gray uniforms, moved down our road, stopping for water or food. Some slept overnight in our barn, but the others pushed on, grateful for whatever we could give them.'"

— Robby Duncan,
Touching Stars

9. Use 1 foundation A and cream print for area 1, green print for area 2, and tan print for area 3 to make **Unit 8**. Make 16 **Unit 8's**.

10. Use 1 foundation B and cream print for area 1, green print for area 2, and tan print for area 3 to make **Unit 9**. Make 16 **Unit 9's**.

11. Use 1 foundation C and purple print for area 1, green print for area 2, and tan print for areas 3 and 4 to make **Unit 10**. Make 16 **Unit 10's**.

12. Use 1 foundation D and purple print for area 1, green print for area 2, and tan print for areas 3 and 4 to make **Unit 11**. Make 16 **Unit 11's**.

13. Sew 1 **Unit 8** and 1 **Unit 10** together to make **Unit 12**. Make 16 **Unit 12's**.

14. Sew 1 **Unit 9** and 1 **Unit 11** together to make **Unit 13**. Make 16 **Unit 13's**.

15. Sew 1 **Unit 12** and 1 **Unit 13** together to make **Unit 14**. Make 16 **Unit 14's**.

16. Sew 4 **Unit 14's** together to make **Block B**. Make 4 **Block B's**.

ASSEMBLING THE QUILT CENTER
*Follow **Piecing**, page 51, and **Pressing**, page 54. Use /4" seam allowances throughout.*

1. Referring to photo, page 18, sew 2 **Block A's** and 1 **Block B** together to make **Row 1**. Make 2 **Rows 1's**.

2. Sew 2 **Block B's** and 1 **Block A** together to make **Row 2**.

3. Sew **Rows** together to complete quilt top center.

ADDING THE BORDERS

1. Sew 1 **inner border** and 1 **outer border** together lengthwise to make 1 **border**. Make 4 **borders**.

2. Mark the center of each edge of quilt top. Mark the center inner edge of each **border**.

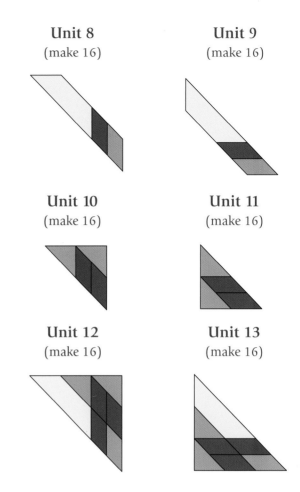

Unit 8 (make 16)   Unit 9 (make 16)

Unit 10 (make 16)   Unit 11 (make 16)

Unit 12 (make 16)   Unit 13 (make 16)

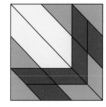

Unit 14 (make 16)

Block B (make 4)

Fig. 1

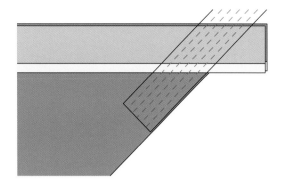

3. Measure across center of quilt top. Beginning at center of **top border**, measure $^1/_2$ the width of the quilt top in both directions and mark.

4. Matching raw edges and marks on **top border** with center and corners of quilt top, pin **top border** to quilt top. Sew **top border** to quilt top, beginning and ending exactly $^1/_4$" from each corner of quilt top. Backstitch at beginning and ending of stitching to reinforce.

5. Repeat Steps 3 – 4 to sew **bottom** and then **side borders** to quilt top.

6. Fold 1 corner of quilt top diagonally with right sides together and matching edges. Aligning ruler with fold, use ruler to mark stitching line as shown in **Fig. 1**. Sew on drawn line, backstitching at beginning and ending of stitching. Turn mitered corner right side up. Check to make sure corner will lie flat with no gaps or puckers. Trim seam allowances to $^1/_4$" and press to one side. Repeat for other corners.

COMPLETING THE QUILT

1. Follow **Quilting**, page 55, to mark, layer, and quilt as desired. Our quilt is machine quilted. The stars are outline quilted. The tan and cream "background" is quilted with outline quilting and curved lines. The inner border is quilted in the ditch and the outer border is quilted with a feather pattern.

2. Follow Making a Hanging Sleeve, page 59, if a hanging sleeve is desired.

3. Cut a 22" square of binding fabric. Follow **Binding**, page 60, to bind quilt using $2^1/_8$"w bias binding with mitered corners.

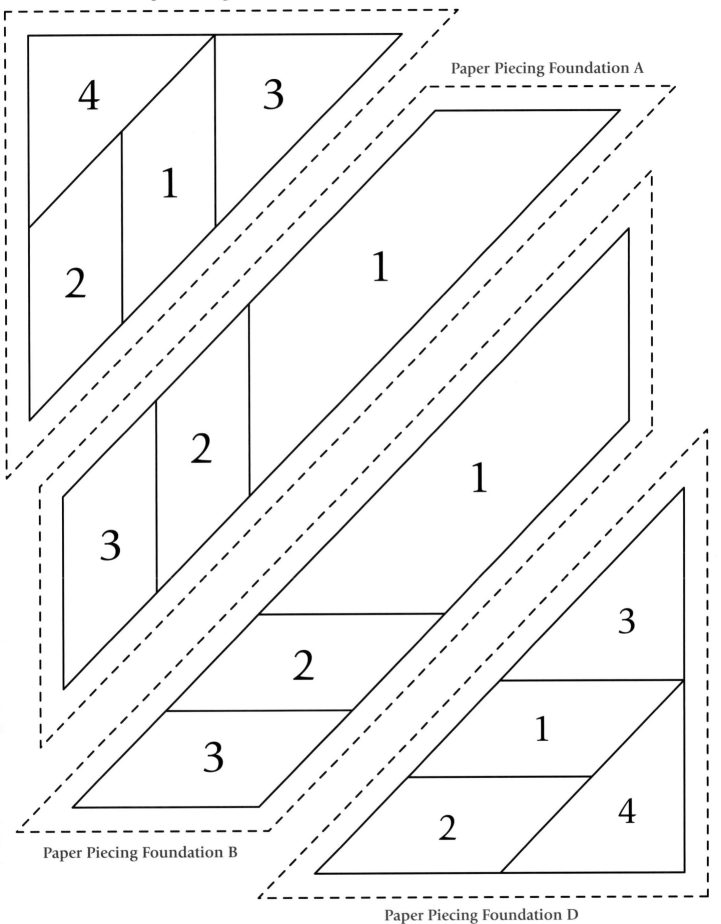

Paper Piecing Foundation C

Paper Piecing Foundation A

Paper Piecing Foundation B

Paper Piecing Foundation D

19

Devil's Puzzle Quilt

*H*elen's right—
"Devil's Puzzle"
is an odd name
for such a useful
quilt block. It's
often combined
with other kinds
of blocks to create
original quilt tops.
And when an entire
quilt top is made
up of these blocks,
it yields a charming
latticework pattern
that sparks ideas
for embellishment.
Wouldn't it be
fun to appliqué
a flowering vine
on a trellis made
from Devil's Puzzle
blocks?

Finished Quilt Size: 74³/₄" x 86³/₄" (190 cm x 220 cm)
Finished Block Size: 12" x 12" (30 cm x 30 cm)

CUTTING OUT THE PIECES

*Follow **Rotary Cutting**, page 50, to cut fabric. Outer borders include an extra 4" of length for "insurance," and will be trimmed after assembling quilt top center. All measurements include $^1/_4$" seam allowances.*

From blue print fabric for inner border:
- Cut 8 **inner border strips** $2^1/_2$"w.

From red print fabric for outer border:
- Cut 2 *lengthwise* **side outer borders** $5^1/_2$" x $80^1/_2$".
- Cut 2 *lengthwise* **top/bottom outer borders** $5^1/_2$" x $78^1/_2$".

YARDAGE REQUIREMENTS

Yardage is based on 43"/44" (109 cm/112 cm) wide fabric.

4 yds (3.7 m) *each* of dark tan print and light tan print fabrics

2 yds (1.8 m) *total* of assorted red print fabrics

2 yds (1.8 m) *total* of assorted blue print fabrics

$^5/_8$ yd (57 cm) of blue print fabric for inner border

$2^3/_8$ yds (2.2 m) of red print fabric for outer border

7 yds (6.4 m) of fabric for backing

1 yd (91 cm) of fabric for binding

You will also need: 83" x 95" (211 cm x 241 cm) piece of batting

"*Helen said, 'When Miranda Duncan's family went in to clean out the old house, they found four hundred Devil's Puzzle blocks in her attic, and not one other block of any other kind. Every single one of them was perfect, too.'*

'Devil's Puzzle?' Gayle asked.

'Oh, it surely has other names, but that's what we called it around here. Never did know why. Can't see anything devilish about it. And once the Depression hit in Shenandoah County, the ladies round here had a lot of quilting bees, and Mrs. Miranda Duncan was the cause of them. A lot of families who needed them had quilts because of her.'"

—from Touching Stars

Unit 1
(make 2 matching)

Unit 2
(make matching)

Block
(make 30)

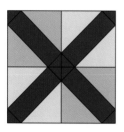

Fig. 1

PAPER PIECING THE BLOCKS

*Photocopy 120 copies of **Paper Piecing Foundation** pattern, page 25. Follow **Paper Piecing**, page 53, to paper piece Blocks. **Note:** For each Block, use 1 red print fabric and 1 blue print fabric.*

1. Use 1 foundation and red print for area 1, dark tan print for areas 2 – 3, and blue print for areas 4 – 5 to make **Unit 1**. Make 2 matching **Unit 1's**.

2. Use 1 foundation and blue print for area 1, light tan print for areas 2 – 3, and red print for areas 4 – 5 to make **Unit 2**. Make 2 matching **Unit 2's**.

3. Sew 2 **Unit 1's** and 2 **Unit 2's** together to make **Block**.

4. Repeat Steps 1 – 3 to make a total of 30 **Blocks**.

ASSEMBLING THE QUILT CENTER

1. Referring to **Quilt Top Diagram**, page 23, sew 5 **Blocks** together to make **Row**. Make 6 **Rows**.

2. Sew **Rows** together to complete quilt top center.

ADDING THE BORDERS

1. Using diagonal seams (**Fig. 1**), sew **inner borders strips** together, end to end, to make 1 continuous border strip.

2. To determine length of **side inner borders**, measure *length* of quilt top center. Cut 2 **side inner borders** from continuous border strip the determined length. Matching centers and corners, sew **side inner borders** to quilt top center.

3. To determine length of **top/bottom inner borders**, measure *width* of quilt top (including added borders). Cut 2 **top/bottom inner borders** from continuous border strip the determined length. Matching centers and corners, sew **top/bottom inner borders** to quilt top.

4. Repeat Steps 2 – 3 to measure, trim, and add **outer borders** to quilt top.

COMPLETING THE QUILT

1. Follow **Quilting**, page 55, to mark, layer, and quilt as desired. Our quilt is machine quilted with twirling leaves and outline stitching in the tan areas. The inner border is stitched in the ditch. Straight lines quilted in the outer border continue the lattice pattern of the blocks.

2. Cut a 29" square of binding fabric. Follow **Binding**, page 60, to bind quilt using 2^{1}/$_{8}$"w bias binding with mitered corners.

Quilt Top Diagram

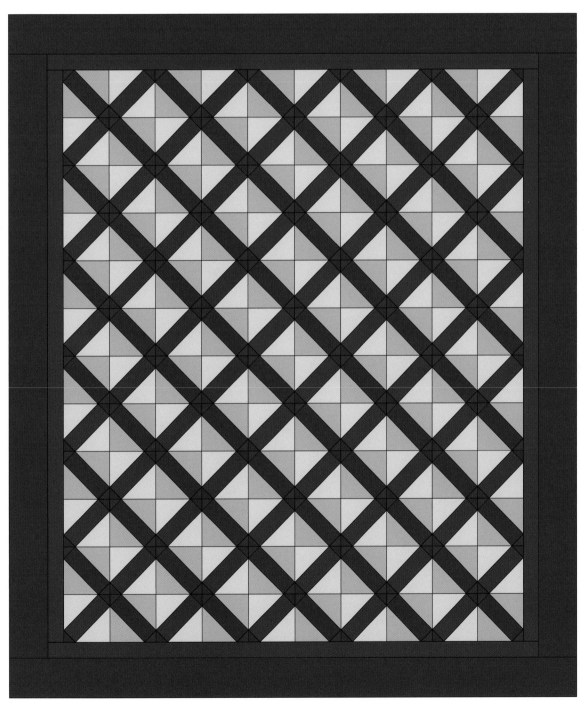

"'I often thought of the quilt my father had carried with him when he rode away to war. The pattern had connecting Xs, like the lattice at the side of our porch, climbing up and across the quilt surface.'"

—Robby Duncan, Touching Stars

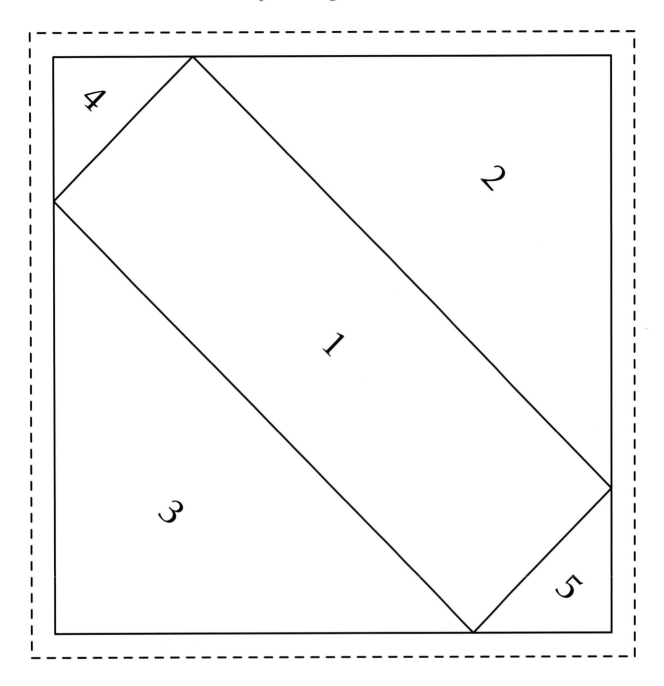

"'Aunt Cora had replied that when lovers signed a letter, they added rows of Xs to stand for kisses. She thought perhaps Pa just wanted to think fondly of my mother when he covered himself at night.'"

—Robby Duncan,
Touching Stars

Ohio Star Quilt

*I*magine buying an older home and discovering the previous owners had left behind vintage quilts! That's what happened over a decade ago when Gayle was exploring the historic house she would convert into a bed-and-breakfast. One of those quilts could very well have been an Ohio Star, a simple pattern that's captured the imagination of quilters for generations.

Finished Quilt Size: 87$^{1}/_{4}$" x 96$^{1}/_{2}$" (222 cm x 245 cm)
Finished Block Size: 8$^{1}/_{4}$" x 8$^{1}/_{4}$" (21 cm x 21 cm)

CUTTING OUT THE PIECES

*Follow **Rotary Cutting**, page 50, to cut fabric. All strips are cut across the width of the fabric. All measurements include $1/4$" seam allowances.*

From white solid fabric:

- Cut 12 strips 4"w. From these strips, cut 112 **large squares** 4" x 4".
- Cut 19 strips $3^1/4$"w. From these strips, cut 224 **small squares** $3^1/4$" x $3^1/4$".
- Cut 16 strips $8^3/4$"w. From these strips, cut 62 **setting squares** $8^3/4$" x $8^3/4$".
- Cut 1 strip 13"w. From this strip, cut 2 squares 13" x 13". Cut squares *twice* diagonally to make 8 **setting triangles**. (You will use 6 and have 2 left over.)
- Cut 2 squares $6^3/4$" x $6^3/4$". Cut squares *once* diagonally to make 4 **corner setting triangles**.

From red solid fabric:

- Cut 12 strips 4"w. From these strips, cut 112 **large squares** 4" x 4".
- Cut 5 strips $3^1/4$"w. From these strips, cut 56 **small squares** $3^1/4$" x $3^1/4$".

"'I got the idea for using quilts as a theme when I found a couple of old ones in the top of a closet,' Gayle said. 'Coupled with the name of the inn, Daughter of the Stars, it made sense. I have those old quilts carefully stored, but since they were mostly red and green, I bring them out at Christmas for a brief showing.'"

—from Touching Stars

YARDAGE REQUIREMENTS

Yardage is based on 43"/44" (109 cm/112 cm) wide fabric.

$8^1/8$ yds (7.4 m) of white solid fabric

2 yds (1.8 m) of red solid fabric

8 yds (7.3 m) of fabric for backing

1 yd (91 cm) of fabric for binding

You will also need:
95" x 105" (241 cm x 267 cm) piece of batting

Template plastic

Air- or water-soluble fabric marking pen

Fig. 1   **Triangle-Squares**
(make 224)

Fig. 2   **Hourglass Units**
(make 224)

Unit 1
(make 112)

Unit 2
(make 56)

Block
(make 56)

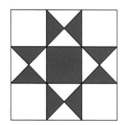

MAKING THE BLOCKS

*Follow **Piecing**, page 51, and **Pressing**, page 54. Use 1/4" seam allowances throughout.*

1. Draw diagonal line (corner to corner) on wrong side of white **large squares**.

2. With right sides together, place 1 white **large square** on top of 1 red **large square**. Stitch seam 1/4" from each side of drawn line (**Fig. 1**).

3. Cut along drawn line and press open to make 2 **Triangle-Squares**. Make 224 **Triangle-Squares**.

4. On half of **Triangles-Squares**, draw a diagonal line (corner to corner and perpendicular to seam).

5. With contrasting fabrics and right sides together, place 1 marked **Triangle-Square** on top of 1 unmarked **Triangle-Square**. Stitch seam 1/4" from each side of drawn line (**Fig. 2**). Cut apart along drawn line and press open to make 2 **Hourglass Units**. Make 224 **Hourglass Units**.

6. Sew 1 **Hourglass Unit** and 2 white **small squares** together to make **Unit 1**. Make 112 **Unit 1's**.

7. Sew 2 **Hourglass Units** and 1 red **small square** together to make **Unit 2**. Make 56 **Unit 2's**.

8. Sew 2 **Unit 1's** and 1 **Unit 2** together to make **Block**. Make 56 **Blocks**.

"Stars had been a favorite of quilters through the centuries, and there had been many to choose from. What could be more perfect for an inn named for the Indian legend that some believed had given the river its name? Daughter of the Stars, the Shenandoah River, where the morning stars had placed the brightest jewels from their crowns."

—from Touching Stars

ASSEMBLING THE QUILT TOP

. Referring to **Assembly Diagram**, sew **Blocks**, **setting squares**, **setting triangles**, and **corner setting triangles** into diagonal **Rows**.

. Sew diagonal **Rows** together to complete quilt top.

COMPLETING THE QUILT

. Follow **Making and Using Templates**, page 51, and use **Scallop** and **Corner Scallop** patterns, page 31, to make scallop templates. Referring to **Fig. 3**, use templates and air- or water-soluble pen to mark scallops on outer **setting squares** and **corner setting triangles**. Do not trim.

. Follow **Quilting**, page 55, to mark, layer, and quilt as desired. Our quilt is hand quilted. The triangles in the Hourglass Units are outline quilted. The squares in the blocks are crosshatch quilted with vertical and horizontal lines, and the setting pieces are crosshatch quilted with diagonal lines.

. To prepare quilt for binding, use a narrow zigzag stitch with a medium stitch length to stitch along top raw edge of quilt top and just outside lines marked in Step 1, stitching through all layers. Trim quilt to $^1/_4$" outside marked line (zigzag stitching should be between marked line and cut line).

. Cut a 31" square of binding fabric. Follow **Making Continuous Bias Binding** and **Attaching Binding to Scalloped Edges**, page 60, to bind quilt using $2^1/_8$"w bias binding.

Assembly Diagram

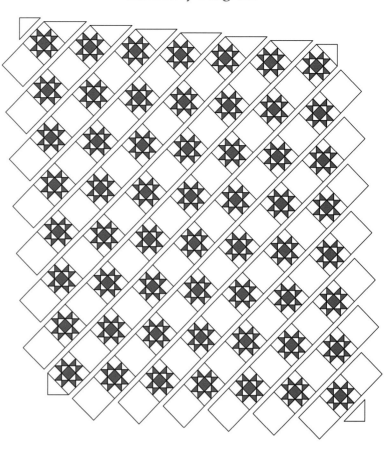

Fig. 3

29

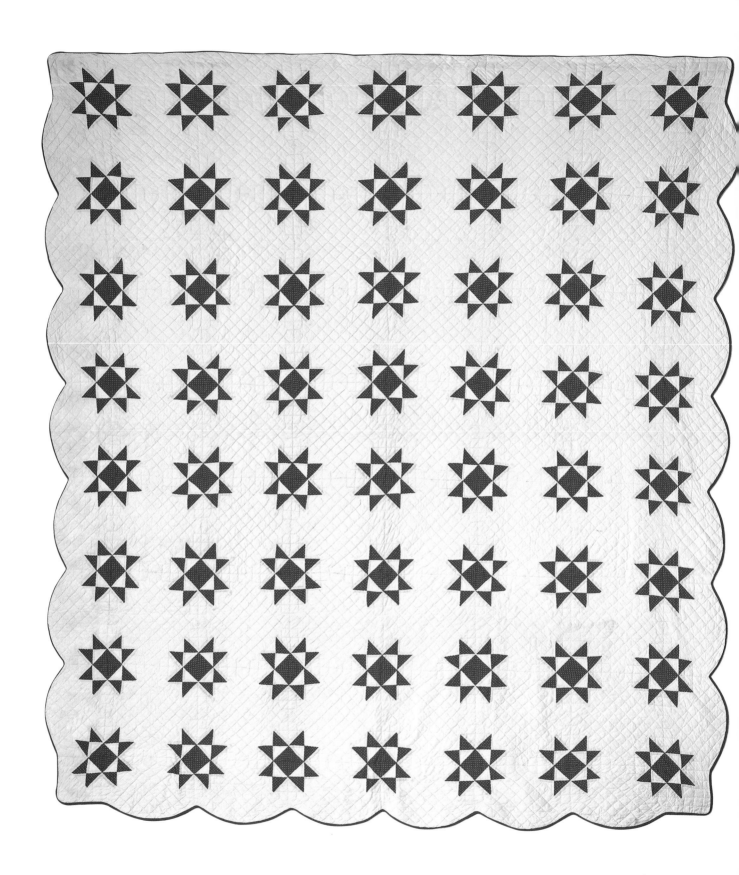

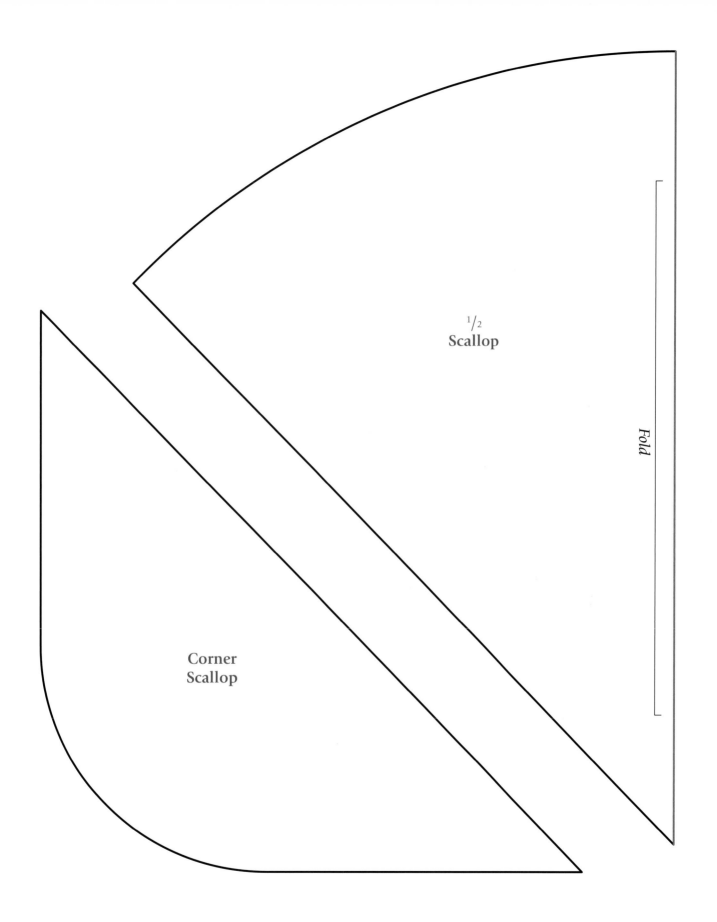

¹/₂
Scallop

Fold

**Corner
Scallop**

Blazing Star Quilt

The impressive Blazing Star is one of several traditional variations on the Lone Star design. It's easy to see why Gayle chose this quilt for the largest room in the inn. The boldness of the spreading star and the soft gradations of color work together to create a pleasant composition.

Finished Quilt Size: 91¹/₄" x 106" (232 cm x 269 cm)

CUTTING OUT THE PIECES

*Follow **Rotary Cutting**, page 50, to cut fabric. All strips are cut across the width of the fabric unless otherwise noted. All measurements include $1/4$" seam allowances.*

From white print fabric:
- Cut 6 strips $11^1/8$"w. From these strips, cut 16 **large background squares** $11^1/8$" x $11^1/8$".
- Cut 1 strip $16^1/4$"w. From this strip, cut 2 squares $16^1/4$" x $16^1/4$". Cut squares *twice* diagonally to make 8 **large background triangles**.
- Cut 2 *lengthwise* **background rectangles** 8" x 73".

From remaining length:
- Cut 10 strips $3^3/8$"w. From these strips, cut 70 **squares** $3^3/8$" x $3^3/8$".
- Cut 3 strips $3^7/8$"w. From these strips, cut 16 **small background squares** $3^7/8$" x $3^7/8$".
- Cut 2 strips $6^1/4$"w. From these strips, cut 4 squares $6^1/4$" x $6^1/4$". Cut squares *twice* diagonally to make 16 **small background triangles**.

From light pink print fabric:
- Cut 15 strips 2"w. Cut strips in half (at fold) to make 30 **wide strips**.

From *each* of turquoise print and dark pink print fabrics:
- Cut 15 strips 2"w. Cut strips in half (at fold) to make 30 **wide strips**.
- Cut 2 strips $1^1/2$"w. Cut strips in half (at fold) to make 4 **narrow strips**.

From light peach print fabric:
- Cut 15 strips 2"w. Cut strips in half (at fold) to make 30 **wide strips**.
- Cut 4 strips $1^1/2$"w. Cut strips in half (at fold) to make 8 **narrow strips**.

From blue print fabric:
- Cut 15 strips 2"w. Cut strips in half (at fold) to make 30 **wide strips**.
- Cut 7 strips $3^3/8$"w. From these strips, cut 70 **squares** $3^3/8$" x $3^3/8$".

From dark peach solid fabric:
- Cut 9 **inner border strips** 3"w.

From peach floral fabric:
- Cut 11 **outer border strips** $4^1/2$"w.

"The Blazing Star was the inn's largest room, with natural maple furniture, sage green walls and an elaborate blazing star quilt of peach, sky blue and green that took up the wall farthest from the windows."

—from Touching Stars

YARDAGE REQUIREMENTS

Yardage is based on 43"/44" (109 cm/112 cm) wide fabric.

$4^7/8$ yds (4.5 m) of white solid fabric

1 yd (91 cm) of light pink print fabric

$1^1/8$ yds (1 m) *each* of turquoise print, dark pink print, and light peach print fabrics

$1^3/4$ yds (1.6 m) of blue print fabric

$7/8$ yd (80 cm) of dark peach solid fabric

$1^5/8$ yds (1.5 m) of peach floral fabric

$8^1/4$ yds (7.5 m) of fabric for backing

1 yd (91 cm) of fabric for binding

You will also need: 99" x 114" (251 cm x 290 cm) piece of batting

6" x 24" acrylic ruler with a 45° angle marking

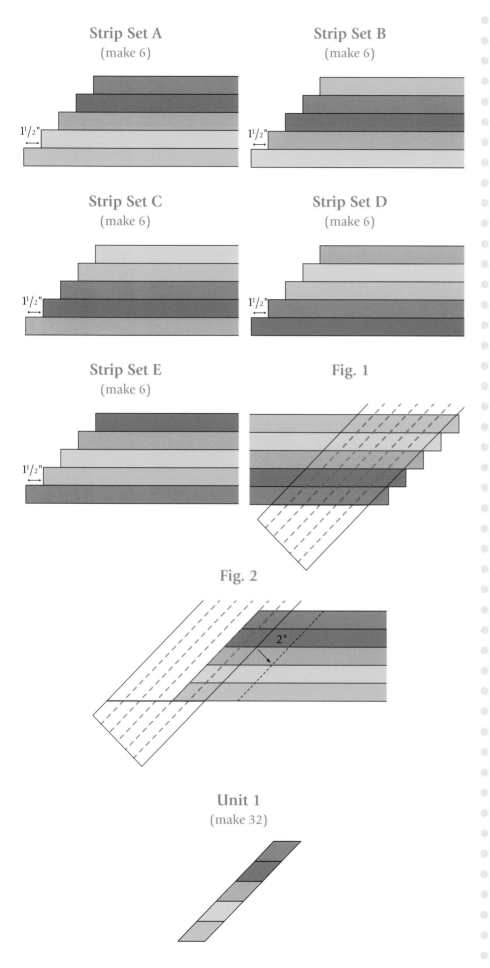

Strip Set A
(make 6)

Strip Set B
(make 6)

1½"

1½"

Strip Set C
(make 6)

Strip Set D
(make 6)

1½"

1½"

Strip Set E
(make 6)

Fig. 1

1½"

Fig. 2

2"

Unit 1
(make 32)

MAKING THE LARGE DIAMOND UNITS

*Follow **Piecing**, page 51, and **Pressing**, page 54. Use ¼" seam allowances throughout.*

1. Sew 5 **wide strips** together lengthwise in color order shown, offsetting strips by 1½" to make **Strip Set A**. Make 6 *each* of **Strip Sets A, B, C, D,** and **E**.

2. Place 1 **Strip Set A** on cutting mat with light pink strip on top. Aligning 45° line on ruler (shown in purple) with bottom edge of **Strip Set A** (**Fig. 1**), trim right edge.

3. Rotate **Strip Set A** so that trimmed edge is on left and dark pink strip is on top. Aligning 45° line on ruler with bottom edge of **Strip Set A**, place ruler on **Strip Set A** so that the 2" mark on ruler is aligned with trimmed edge (**Fig. 2**). Cut on right side of ruler to make **Unit 1**. Moving ruler to right, aligning 2" mark with cut edge, and cutting on right side of ruler, continue making **Unit 1's**. Repeat with remaining **Strip Set A's** to make a *total* of 32 **Unit 1's**.

4. From **Strip Set B's**, cut 32 **Unit 2's**.

5. From **Strip Set C's**, cut 32 **Unit 3's**.

6. From **Strip Set D's**, cut 32 **Unit 4's**.

7. From **Strip Set E's**, cut 32 **Unit 5's**.

8. Sew 2 **narrow strips** together lengthwise in color order shown, offsetting strips by 1" to make **Strip Set F**. Make 4 *each* of **Strip Sets F** and **G**.

9. Place 1 **Strip Set F** on cutting mat with dark pink strip on top. Aligning 45° line on ruler (shown in purple) with bottom edge of **Strip Set F** (**Fig. 3**), trim right edge.

10. Rotate **Strip Set F** so that trimmed edge is on left and light peach strip is on top. Aligning 45° line on ruler with bottom edge of **Strip Set F**, place ruler on **Strip Set F** so that the 1¹/₂" mark on ruler is aligned with trimmed edge (**Fig. 4**). Cut on right side of ruler to make **Unit 6**. Moving ruler to right, aligning 1¹/₂" mark with cut edge, and cutting on right side of ruler, continue making **Unit 1's**. Repeat with remaining **Strip Set F's** to make a *total* of 32 **Unit 6's**.

11. From **Strip Set G's**, cut 32 **Unit 7's**.

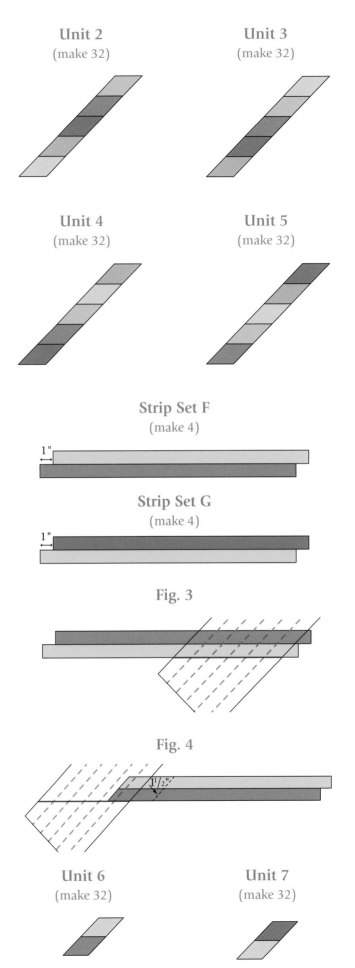

Unit 2
(make 32)

Unit 3
(make 32)

Unit 4
(make 32)

Unit 5
(make 32)

Strip Set F
(make 4)

1"

Strip Set G
(make 4)

1"

Fig. 3

Fig. 4

1¹/₂"

Unit 6
(make 32)

Unit 7
(make 32)

35

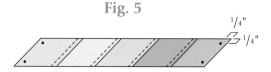

Fig. 5

Fig. 6

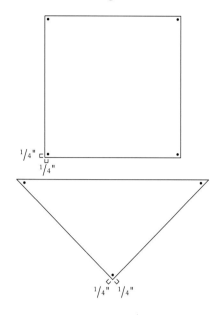

1/4"
1/4"

1/4" 1/4"

Fig. 7

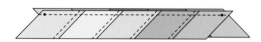

Large Diamond Unit
(make 32)

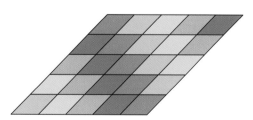

Small Diamond Unit
(make 32)

MARKING THE ¹/₄" SEAM ALLOWANCES

Because of the diamond shapes, marking seam allowances at corners of Units and background pieces will allow for more accurate piecing.

1. On wrong side of each **Unit 1 – 7**, make a dot with pencil ¹/₄" from edges in each corner (**Fig. 5**).

2. On wrong side of each **large** and **small background square** and **large** and **small background triangle**, mark a dot with pencil ¹/₄" from edges in each corner (**Fig 6**).

MAKING THE DIAMOND UNITS

1. Sew 1 **Unit 1**, 1 **Unit 2**, 1 **Unit 3**, 1 **Unit 4**, and 1 **Unit 5** together in order shown to make **Large Diamond Unit**. *Note: When making Large Diamond Units, refer to Fig. 7 and match dots and long edges of Units.* Make 32 **Large Diamond Units**.

2. In the same manner, sew 1 **Unit 6** and 1 **Unit 7** together to make **Small Diamond Unit**. Make 32 **small Diamond Units**.

ASSEMBLING THE QUILT TOP CENTER

*Follow **Working with In-Set Seams**, page 53, to assemble quilt top center. Refer to **Quilt Top Diagram**, page 39, for placement.*

1. Sew 2 **Large Diamond Units** together make **Unit 8**. Make 4 **Unit 8's**.

2. Sew 4 **Unit 8's** together to make **Large Star**.

3. Sew 8 **large background squares** to **Large Star** to make **Unit 9**.

4. Sew 3 **Large Diamond Units** together to make **Unit 10**. Make 8 **Unit 10's**.

5. Sew 8 **Unit 10's** to **Unit 9** to make **Star Blaze**.

6. Sew 8 **large background triangles** and then 8 **large background squares** to **Star Blaze** to make **Unit 11**.

7. Sew 8 **Small Diamond Units** together to make **Small Star**. Make 4 **Small Stars**.

8. Sew 4 **small background triangles** and then 4 **small background squares** to each **Small Star** to make 4 **Small Star Blocks**. *Note: Small background triangles and squares are over-sized.* Centering design, trim **Small Star Blocks** to $10^5/8$" x $10^5/8$".

9. Sew 1 **Small Star Block** to each corner of **Unit 11** to make **Unit 12**.

10. Matching centers and corners, sew **background rectangles** to top and bottom edges of **Unit 12** to complete quilt top center.

Unit 8
(make 4)

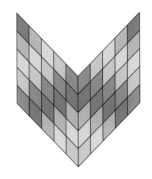

Large Star

Unit 10
(make 8)

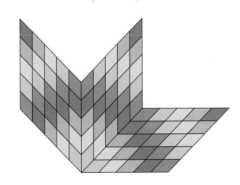

Small Star
(make 4)

Small Star Block
(make 4)

Fig. 8

Triangle-Squares

(make 140)

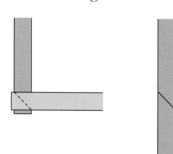

Fig. 9

MAKING THE SAWTOOTH BORDER

1. Draw a diagonal line (corner to corner) on wrong side of each white **square**. With right sides together, place 1 white **square** on top of 1 blue **square**. Stitch seam 1/4" from each side of drawn line (**Fig. 8**).

2. Cut along drawn line and press seam allowances toward blue fabric to make 2 **Triangle-Squares**. Make 140 **Triangle-Squares**.

3. Sew 31 **Triangle-Squares** together to make **top sawtooth border**. Repeat to make **bottom sawtooth border**.

4. Sew 39 **Triangle-Squares** together to make **side sawtooth border**. Make 2 **side sawtooth borders**.

ADDING THE BORDERS

1. Using diagonal seams (**Fig. 9**), sew inner borders strips together, end to end, to make 1 continuous border strip.

2. To determine length of **side inner borders**, measure *length* of quilt top center. Cut 2 **side inner borders** from continuous border strip the determined length. Matching centers and corners, sew **side inner borders** to quilt top center.

3. To determine length of **top/bottom inner borders**, measure *width* of quilt top (including added borders). Cut 2 **top/bottom inner borders** from continuous border strip the determined length. Matching centers and corners, sew **top/bottom inner borders** to quilt top.

4. Matching centers and corners, sew **top**, **bottom**, and then **side sawtooth borders** to quilt top. *Note: Length of sawtooth borders may be adjusted if needed by making some of the seams between Triangle-Squares slightly smaller or larger.*

5. Repeat Steps 1 – 3 to add **outer borders** using **outer border strips** to complete quilt top.

"*The* inn was furnished with simple furniture, some antiques and some reproductions that gently suggested life as the former residents might have lived it. The quilts pulled everything together. An appreciative guest had shared her own theory about Gayle's love affair with quilts. Anyone describing a quilt—comfortable, traditional, warm, inviting—could well be describing Gayle, herself."

—from Touching Stars

COMPLETING THE QUILT

1. Follow **Quilting**, page 55, to mark, layer, and quilt as desired. Our quilt is hand quilted. The stars and sawtooth border are filled with outline quilting and the background and outer border are quilted with feather and channel patterns. A diamond pattern is quilted in the inner border.

2. Cut a 31" square of binding fabric. Follow **Binding**, page 60, to bind quilt using $2^1/_8$"w bias binding with mitered corners.

Quilt Top Diagram

The Gift Shop

The Daughter of the Stars Inn offers a summer entertainment series featuring local crafters. Valley artists demonstrate and instruct their specialties at the inn and sell their wares in Gayle's small gift shop. Some of the most popular items at the shop are quilted items made by Helen and the SCC Bee quilters.

SEVEN SISTERS FRAMED BLOCK

Finished Bound Block Size: $12^3/8$" x $10^3/4$"
(31 cm x 27 cm)
Note: We recommend hand piecing the Seven Sisters Block.

CUTTING OUT THE PIECES

*Follow **Making and Using Templates**, page 51, to cut fabric from templates. Patterns for templates are on page 42.*

From cream fabric:
- Cut 1 **bias strip for binding** $2^1/8$" x 50", pieced as necessary.
- Cut 18 **A's** from template.
- Cut 6 **B's** from template.

From *each* brown print and blue print fabrics:
- Cut 21 **A's** from template.

"Gayle had fallen in love with the Touching Stars pattern and the quilt top at first sight, as well as the dozens of varied star blocks the quilters had pieced and quilted to sell in her shop as potholders or table toppers."

—from Touching Stars

YARDAGE REQUIREMENTS

Yardage is based on 43"/44" (109 cm/112 cm) wide fabric.

$1/2$ yd (46 cm) of cream print fabric (includes binding)

$1/8$ yd (11 cm) *each* of brown print and blue print fabrics

15" x 13" (38 cm x 33 cm) piece of fabric for backing

You will also need: 15" x 13" (38 cm x 33 cm) piece of batting

Frame with an opening of approximately $13^1/2$" x $13^1/2$" (34 cm x 34 cm)*

Mat board*

Double-sided masking tape*

Framing spacers*

*We used an inexpensive purchased frame. You may choose to have your quilt block custom framed.

Unit 1
(make 21)

Star
(make 7)

Unit 2

Unit 3
Assembly

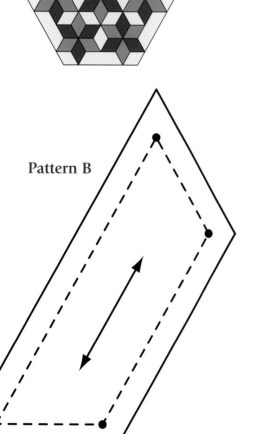

Seven Sisters Block

Pattern B

MAKING THE BLOCK

*Follow **Hand Piecing**, page 51. Press seam allowances open.*

1. Sew 1 **blue A** and 1 **brown A** together to make **Unit 1**. Make 21 **Unit 1's**.

2. Sew 3 **Unit 1's** together to make **Star**. Make 7 **Stars**.

3. Sew 1 **Star** and 6 cream **A's** together to make **Unit 2**.

4. Referring to **Unit 3 Assembly** diagram, sew 1 cream **A** to each **Star** and then sew **Stars** to **Unit 2** to make **Unit 3**.

5. Sew **Unit 3**, 6 cream **A's**, and 6 cream **B's** together to make **Seven Sisters Block**.

COMPLETING THE FRAMED BLOCK

1. Layer backing (right side down), batting, and Block (centered and right side up). Follow **Quilting**, page 55, to baste and quilt as desired. Our Block is hand outline quilted.

2. Press **bias binding strip** in half lengthwise. Use strip and follow **Attaching Binding with Mitered Corners**, page 61, to bind Block.

3. If using a purchased frame, cut a matching mat board for the background and use double-sided masking tape to secure Block to mat board. Use spacers to prevent glass from flattening Block.

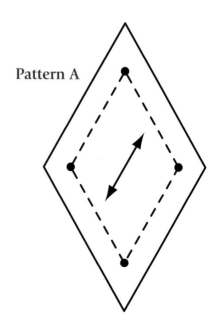

Pattern A

RISING STAR TABLE RUNNER

Finished Table Runner Size: 16" x 52" (41 cm x 132 cm)
Finished Block Size: 12" x 12" (30 cm x 30 cm)

CUTTING OUT THE PIECES

Follow Rotary Cutting, page 50, to cut fabric. All strips are cut across the width of the fabric unless otherwise noted. All measurements include $^1/_4$" seam allowances.

From floral fabric:
- Cut 1 *lengthwise* **backing** $18^1/_2$" x $54^1/_2$".
- Cut 2 *lengthwise* **strips** $2^1/_2$" x $36^1/_2$".
- Cut 1 square $12^1/_4$" x $12^1/_4$". Cut square *once* diagonally to make 2 **triangles**.

From yellow print fabric:
- Cut 1 strip $3^1/_2$"w. From this strip, cut 3 **center squares** $3^1/_2$" x $3^1/_2$".
- Cut 2 strips 2"w. From these strips, cut 24 **small squares** 2" x 2".

From red print fabric:
- Cut 3 strips $3^1/_2$"w. From these strips, cut 16 **large squares** $3^1/_2$" x $3^1/_2$" and 8 **large rectangles** $3^1/_2$" x $6^1/_2$".
- Cut 1 strip 2"w. From this strip, cut 4 **small squares** 2" x 2" and 4 **small rectangles** 2" x $3^1/_2$".

From blue print fabric:
- Cut 3 strips $3^1/_2$"w. From these strips, cut 20 **large squares** $3^1/_2$" x $3^1/_2$" and 4 **large rectangles** $3^1/_2$" x $6^1/_2$".
- Cut 2 strips 2"w. From these strips, cut 8 **small squares** 2" x 2" and 8 **small rectangles** 2" x $3^1/_2$".

YARDAGE REQUIREMENTS

Yardage is based on 43"/44" (109 cm/112 cm) wide fabric.

$1^3/_4$ yds (1.6 m) of floral fabric (includes backing)

$^1/_4$ yd (23 cm) of yellow print fabric

$^1/_2$ yd (46 cm) of red print fabric

$^1/_2$ yd (46 cm) of blue print fabric

You will also need: $18^1/_2$" x $54^1/_2$" (47 cm x 138 cm) piece of batting

Fig. 1

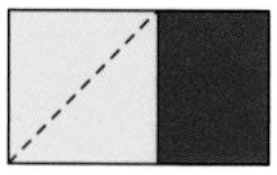

Fig. 2

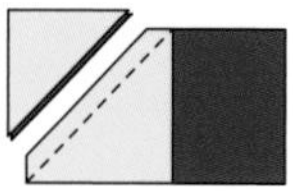

Fig. 3

Fig. 4

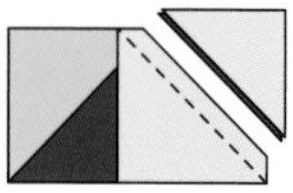

Small Flying Geese Unit A
(make 8)

Small Flying Geese Unit B
(make 4)

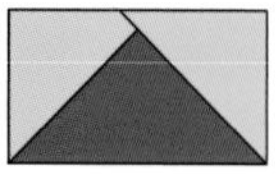

Large Flying Geese Unit A
(make 8)

Large Flying Geese Unit B
(make 4)

Unit 1
(make 2)

Unit 2

Unit 3

Unit 4
(make 2)

MAKING THE BLOCKS

*Follow **Piecing**, page 51, and **Pressing**, page 54. Use ¹/₄" seam allowances throughout.*

1. With right sides together, place 1 yellow **small square** on 1 end of 1 blue **small rectangle** and stitch diagonally (**Fig. 1**). Trim ¹/₄" from stitching line (**Fig. 2**). Open up and press (**Fig. 3**).

2. Place another yellow **small square** on opposite end of **small rectangle**. Stitch and trim as shown in **Fig. 4**. Open up and press to make **Small Flying Geese Unit A**. Make 8 **Small Flying Geese Unit A's**.

3. Using yellow **small squares** and red **small rectangles**, make 4 **Small Flying Geese Unit B's**.

4. Using blue **large squares** and red **large rectangles**, make 8 **Large Flying Geese Unit A's**.

5. Using red **large squares** and blue **large rectangles**, make 4 **Large Flying Geese Unit B's**.

6. Sew 1 **Small Flying Geese Unit A** and 2 blue **small squares** together to make **Unit 1**. Make 2 **Unit 1's**.

7. Sew 2 **Small Flying Geese Unit A's** and 1 yellow **center square** together to make **Unit 2**.

8. Sew 2 **Unit 1's** and 1 **Unit 2** together to make **Unit 3**.

9. Sew 1 **Large Flying Geese Unit A** and 2 red **large squares** together to make **Unit 4**. Make 2 **Unit 4's**.

0. Sew 2 **Large Flying Geese Unit A's** and 1 **Unit 3** together to make **Unit 5**.

1. Sew 2 **Unit 4's** and 1 **Unit 5** together to make **Block A**.

2. Repeat Steps 6 – 11 to make a second **Block A**.

3. Repeat Steps 6 – 11 changing red to blue and blue to red to make **Block B**.

ASSEMBLING THE TABLE RUNNER TOP

. Sew **Blocks** together to make table runner top center.

. Sew 1 **strip** to each long side of table runner top center.

. Sew 1 **triangle** to each short side of table runner top center.

COMPLETING THE TABLE RUNNER

. Layer batting, backing (right side up), and table runner top (centered and right side down). Leaving an opening on 1 long edge for turning, sew layers together $1/4$" from edges of table runner top. Trim backing and batting even with table runner top; clip corners.

. Turn table runner right side out and sew opening closed.

. Follow **Quilting**, page 55, to mark, layer, and quilt as desired. Our table runner is quilted in the ditch and straight lines are quilted in the triangles.

Unit 5

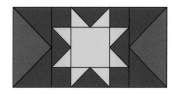

Block A

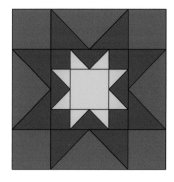

Block B

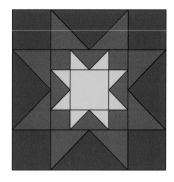

Table Runner Diagram

YARDAGE REQUIREMENTS

Yardage is based on 43"/44" (109 cm/112 cm) wide fabric.

$^5/_8$ yd (57 cm) of floral fabric (includes pillow back)

$^1/_8$ yd (11 cm) of yellow print fabric

$^1/_4$ yd (23 cm) of red print fabric

$^1/_8$ yd (11 cm) of blue print fabric

$^5/_8$ yd (57 cm) of muslin fabric

You will also need:
$18^1/_2$" x $18^1/_2$" (47 cm x 47 cm) piece of batting

16" x 16" (41 cm x 41 cm) pillow form

Fig. 1

Fig. 2

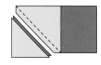

Fig. 3

MEMORY BLOCK PILLOW
Photo on page 43.

Finished Pillow Size: 16" x 16" (41 cm x 41 cm)

CUTTING OUT THE PIECES
*Follow **Rotary Cutting**, page 50, to cut fabric. All strips are cut across the width of the fabric. All measurements include $^1/_4$" seam allowances.*

From floral fabric:
- Cut 1 strip $2^1/_2$"w. From this strip, cut 8 **small squares** $2^1/_2$" x $2^1/_2$" and 4 **rectangles** $2^1/_2$" x $4^1/_2$".
- Cut 2 **top/bottom borders** $2^1/_2$" x $16^1/_2$".
- Cut 2 **side borders** $2^1/_2$" x $12^1/_2$".
- Cut 2 **pillow back rectangles** $16^1/_2$" x $10^1/_4$".
- Cut 1 **large square** $4^1/_2$" x $4^1/_2$".

From yellow print fabric:
- Cut 1 strip $2^1/_2$"w. From this strip, cut 8 **small squares** $2^1/_2$" x $2^1/_2$".

From red print fabric:
- Cut 1 strip $2^7/_8$"w. From this strip, cut 4 **medium squares** $2^7/_8$" x $2^7/_8$".
- Cut 1 strip $2^1/_2$"w. From this strip, cut 4 **small squares** $2^1/_2$" x $2^1/_2$" and 4 **rectangles** $2^1/_2$" x $4^1/_2$".

From blue print fabric:
- Cut 4 **medium squares** $2^7/_8$" x $2^7/_8$".
- Cut 4 **small squares** $2^1/_2$" x $2^1/_2$".

From muslin fabric:
- Cut 1 square $18^1/_2$" x $18^1/_2$" for **backing**.

MAKING THE PILLOW TOP
*Follow **Piecing**, page 51, and **Pressing**, page 54. Use $^1/_4$" seam allowances throughout.*

1. With right sides together, place 1 yellow **small square** on 1 end of 1 floral **rectangle** and stitch diagonally (**Fig. 1**). Trim $^1/_4$" from stitching line (**Fig. 2**). Open up and press (**Fig. 3**).

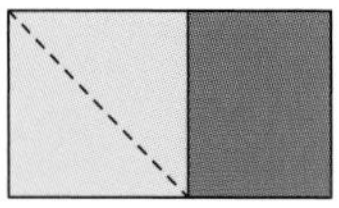

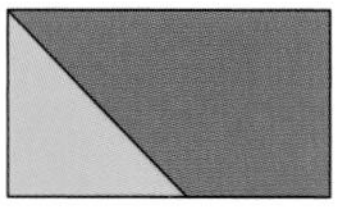

2. Place another yellow **small square** on opposite end of **rectangle**. Stitch and trim as shown in **Fig. 4**. Open up and press to make **Flying Geese Unit A**. Make 4 **Flying Geese Unit A's**.

3. Using floral **small squares** and red **rectangles**, make 4 **Flying Geese Unit B's**.

4. Sew 1 **Flying Geese Unit A** and 1 **Flying Geese Unit B** together make **Unit 1**. Make 4 **Unit 1's**.

5. Draw diagonal line (corner to corner) on wrong side of red **medium squares**.

6. With right sides together, place 1 red **medium square** on top of 1 blue **medium square**. Stitch seam $^1/_4$" from each side of drawn line (**Fig. 5**).

7. Cut along drawn line and press open to make 2 **Triangle-Squares**. Make 8 **Triangle-Squares**.

8. Sew 2 **Triangle-Squares**, 1 red **small square**, and 1 blue **small square** together to make **Unit 2**. Make 4 **Unit 2's**.

9. Sew 1 **Unit 1** and 2 **Unit 2's** together to make **Unit 3**. Make 2 **Unit 3's**.

10. Sew 2 **Unit 1's** and **large square** together to make **Unit 4**.

11. Sew 2 **Unit 3's** and 1 **Unit 4** together to make **Memory Block**.

12. Sew **side** and then **top/bottom borders** to **Block** to complete pillow top.

Fig. 4

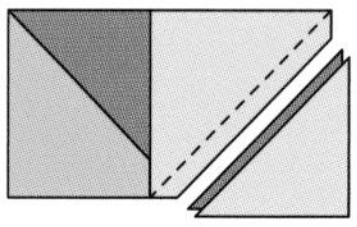

Flying Geese Unit A
(make 4)

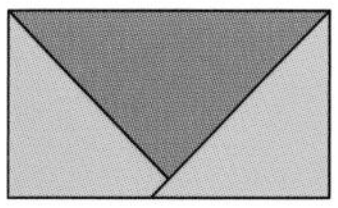

Flying Geese Unit B
(make 4)

Unit 1
(make 4)

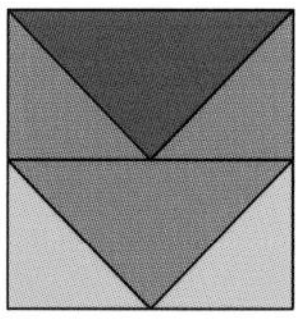

Fig. 5

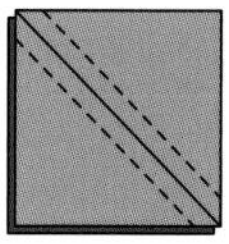

Triangle-Squares
(make 8)

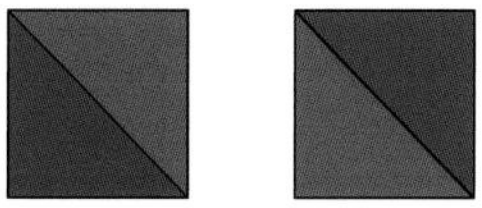

Unit 2
(make 4)

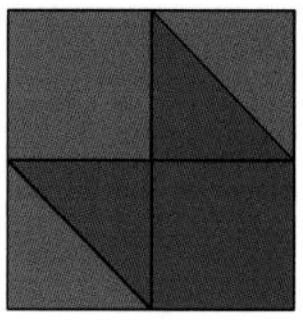

Unit 3
(make 2)

Unit 4

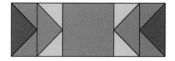

Memory Block

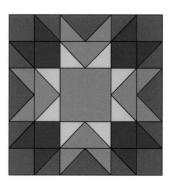

Pillow Diagram

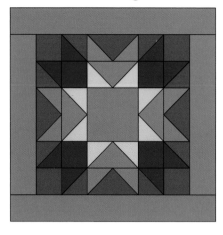

COMPLETING THE PILLOW

1. Layer muslin **backing**, batting, and pillow top (centered and right side up). Follow **Quilting**, page 55, to baste and quilt as desired. Our pillow is quilted in the ditch.

2. Trim backing and batting even with pillow top.

3. On each **pillow back rectangle**, press 1 long edge ¹/₄" to the wrong side; press ¹/₄" to the wrong side again and stitch in place.

4. Overlap hemmed edges of **pillow back rectangles**, right sides facing up, to form a 16¹/₂" x 16¹/₂" square for pillow back. Baste **pillow back rectangles** together at overlap.

5. With right sides facing, pin pillow top and pillow back together. Sew around pillow. Remove basting, clip corners, turn, and press. Insert pillow form.

YARDAGE REQUIREMENTS
Yardage is based on 43"/44" (109 cm/112 cm) wide fabric.

¹/₂ yd (46 cm) of floral fabric

¹/₈ yd (11 cm) of yellow print fabric

¹/₈ yd (11 cm) of red print fabric

¹/₈ yd (11 cm) of blue print fabric

You will also need:
Two 10¹/₂" x 10¹/₂" (27 cm x 27 cm) squares of cotton batting

SLANTED DIAMONDS POTHOLDER
Photo on page 43.

Finished Potholder Size: 8¹/₂" x 8¹/₂" (22 cm x 22 cm)

CUTTING OUT THE PIECES
*Follow **Rotary Cutting**, page 50, to cut fabric. All strips are cut across the width of the fabric. All measurements include ¹/₄" seam allowances.*

From floral fabric:
- Cut 1 **binding strip** 2¹/₈"w.
- Cut 1 **backing square** 10¹/₂" x 10¹/₂".
- Cut 1 **handle strip** 1" x 3¹/₂".

From yellow print fabric:
- Cut 1 strip 2⁷/₈"w. From this strips, cut 8 **squares** 2⁷/₈" x 2⁷/₈".

From red print fabric:
- Cut 1 strip 2⁷/₈"w. From this strips, cut 4 **squares** 2⁷/₈" x 2⁷/₈".

From blue print fabric:
- Cut 1 strip 2⁷/₈"w. From this strips, cut 4 **squares** 2⁷/₈" x 2⁷/₈".

MAKING THE POTHOLDER TOP

*Follow **Piecing**, page 51, and **Pressing**, page 54. Use /4" seam allowances throughout.*

1. Draw diagonal line (corner to corner) on wrong side of yellow **squares**.

2. With right sides together, place 1 yellow **square** on top of 1 blue **square**. Stitch seam $1/4$" from each side of drawn line (**Fig. 1**).

3. Cut along drawn line and press open to make 2 **Triangle-Square A's**. Make 8 **Triangle-Square A's**.

4. Using red **squares** and remaining yellow **squares**, make 8 **Triangle-Square B's**.

5. Sew 4 **Triangle-Square A's** together to make **Unit 1**. Make 2 **Unit 1's**.

6. Sew 4 **Triangle-Square B's** together to make **Unit 2**. Make 2 **Unit 2's**.

7. Sew 2 **Unit 1's** and 2 **Unit 2's** together to make **Slanted Diamond Block**.

COMPLETING THE POTHOLDER

1. Layer backing (right side down), 2 batting squares, and **Block** (centered and right side up). Follow **Quilting**, page 55, to baste and quilt as desired. Our potholder is quilted in the ditch.

2. Trim backing and batting even with **Block**.

3. With right sides together, fold **handle strip** in half *lengthwise*. Sew long edges together; turn handle right side out. Matching raw edges, baste handle to 1 corner of potholder.

4. Press **binding strip** in half lengthwise. Use strip and follow **Attaching Binding with Mitered Corners**, page 61, to bind potholder.

Fig. 1

Triangle-Square A's
(make 8)

Triangle-Square B's
(make 8)

Unit 1
(make 2)

Unit 2
(make 2)

Slanted Diamond Block

Potholder Diagram

49

General Instructions

To make your quilting easier and more enjoyable, we encourage you to carefully read all of the general instructions, study the color photographs, and familiarize yourself with the individual project instructions before beginning a project

Fig. 1

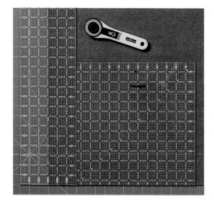

Fig. 2

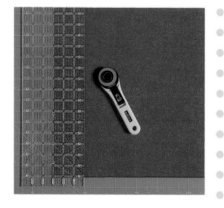

Fig. 3

FABRICS

SELECTING FABRICS

Choose high-quality, medium-weight 100% cotton fabrics. All-cotton fabrics hold a crease better, fray less, and are easier to quilt than cotton/polyester blends.

Yardage requirements listed for each project are based on 43"/44" wide fabric with a "usable" width of 40" after shrinkage and trimming selvages. Actual usable width will probably vary slightly from fabric to fabric. Our recommended yardage lengths should be adequate for occasional re-squaring of fabric when many cuts are required.

PREPARING FABRICS

We recommend that all fabrics be washed, dried, and pressed before cutting. If fabrics are not pre-washed, washing the finished quilt will cause shrinkage and give it a more "antiqued" look and feel. Bright and dark colors, which may run, should always be washed before cutting. After washing and drying fabric, fold lengthwise with wrong sides together and matching selvages.

ROTARY CUTTING

Rotary cutting has brought speed and accuracy to quiltmaking by allowing quilters to easily cut strips of fabric and then cut those strips into smaller pieces.

- Place fabric on work surface with fold closest to you.

- Cut all strips from the selvage-to-selvage width of the fabric unless otherwise indicated in project instructions.

- Square left edge of fabric using rotary cutter and rulers (**Figs. 1 – 2**).

- To cut each strip required for a project, place ruler over cut edge of fabric, aligning desired marking on ruler with cut edge; make cut (**Fig. 3**).

- When cutting several strips from a single piece of fabric, it is important to make sure that cuts remain at a perfect right angle to the fold; square fabric as needed.

MAKING AND USING TEMPLATES

This book includes patterns for 2 types of templates: templates for cutting scalloped edges (**Ohio Star Quilt**); and piecing templates (**Seven Sisters Framed Block**). Our piecing template patterns have two lines – a solid cutting line and a dashed line showing the 1/4" seam allowance.

SCALLOP TEMPLATE

1. To make a scallop template from pattern, use a permanent fine-point pen to carefully trace pattern onto template plastic. Cut out template along inner edge of drawn line. Follow project instructions to cut scalloped edges of quilt using templates.

PIECING TEMPLATE

1. To make a piecing template from pattern, use a permanent fine-point pen and a ruler to carefully trace pattern onto template plastic. For hand piecing, trace inner dashed line (finished size). Transfer any alignment and grain line markings. Cut out template along inner edge of drawn line. Check template against original pattern for accuracy.

2. Place template face down on wrong side of fabric aligning grain line on template with straight grain of fabric. Use a sharp fabric-marking pencil to draw around template. Transfer all alignment markings to fabric. Add 1/4" seam allowances outside drawn line and cut out fabric piece using scissors or rotary cutting equipment.

PIECING

Precise cutting, followed by accurate piecing, will ensure that all pieces of quilt top fit together well.

HAND PIECING

- Matching right sides, pin two pieces together, using pins to mark corners.

- Use Running Stitch to sew pieces together along drawn line, backstitching at beginning and end of seam.

- Do not extend stitches into seam allowances.

- Run five or six stitches onto needle before pulling needle through fabric.

- To add stability, backstitch every 3/4" to 1".

"'*You* work so diligently on that quilt, although so many others are in evidence here,' Blackjack said. 'It's almost as if you need two dozen for each bed in your house.'

'There'll come a time when my fingers will be stiff and my eyes poor. Then I'll still have quilts to keep me warm,' Miranda replied."

—from Touching Stars

MACHINE PIECING

- Set sewing machine stitch length for approximately 11 stitches per inch.

- Use neutral-colored general-purpose sewing thread (not quilting thread) in needle and in bobbin.

- An accurate $1/4$" seam allowance is *essential*. Presser feet that are $1/4$" wide are available for most sewing machines.

- When piecing, always place pieces right sides together and match raw edges; pin if necessary.

- Chain piecing saves time and will usually result in more accurate piecing.

- Trim away points of seam allowances that extend beyond edges of sewn pieces.

Sewing Strip Sets

When there are several strips to assemble into a strip set, first sew strips together into pairs, then sew pairs together to form strip set. To help avoid distortion, sew seams in opposite directions (**Fig. 4**).

Sewing Across Seam Intersections

When sewing across intersection of two seams, place pieces right sides together and match seams exactly, making sure seam allowances are pressed in opposite directions (**Fig. 5**).

Sewing Sharp Points

To ensure sharp points when joining triangular or diagonal pieces, stitch across the center of the "X" (shown in pink) formed on wrong side by previous seams (**Fig. 6**).

Fig. 4

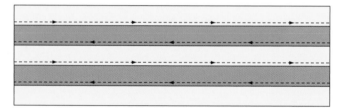

Fig. 5

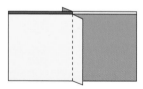

Fig. 6

WORKING WITH IN-SET SEAMS

Project instructions call for marking dots on units and setting pieces ¹/₄" from edges at corners. This will make sewing in-set seams easier and more accurate.

1. When sewing two diamond-shaped pieces together, place pieces right sides together, carefully matching edges; pin. Stitch seam from dot to dot, backstitching at dots (**Fig. 7**); clip threads.

2. For best results, add background triangles, then background squares to diamond sections (**Fig. 8**).

3. To sew first seam, match right sides and pin triangle or square to diamond on the left. Stitch seam from dot to dot, backstitching at dots; clip threads (**Fig. 9**).

4. To sew second seam, pivot added triangle or square to match raw edges of next diamond. Beginning at dot, take two or three stitches, then backstitch, making sure not to backstitch into previous seam allowance. Continue stitching to next dot and backstitch (**Fig. 10**).

PAPER PIECING

Foundation patterns for paper piecing are included with individual projects. Photocopy the number of patterns called for in project instructions.

*Always stitch seams with the paper foundation on top, right side up. Once a Unit is paper pieced, the pattern and fabric pieces will be **wrong sides together**.*

Very important: Shorten stitch length to 18 stitches per inch to make paper removal easier.

As you press, use a dry iron (steam will curl the paper).
Note: Some photocopied patterns may smear when ironed. Test your patterns and use a pressing cloth if needed.

Fig. 7

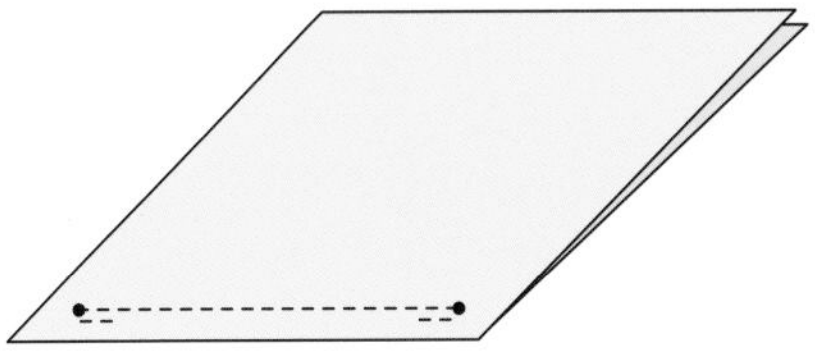

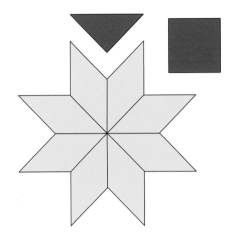

Fig. 8

Fig. 9

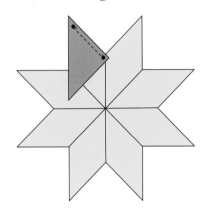

Fig. 10

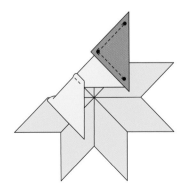

53

Fig. 11

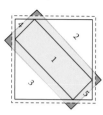

Fig. 12

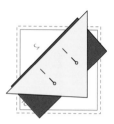

Fig. 13

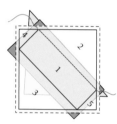

Fig. 14

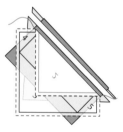

Fig. 15

Fig. 16

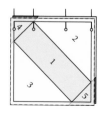

1. Rough cut a piece of fabric for area 1 at least ¹/₂" larger on all sides than area 1 on foundation. With wrong sides together, cover area 1 of foundation with fabric piece for area 1. Hold foundation up to lamp or bright window to make sure fabric covers area 1 and area 1 seam allowances. Pin or glue (using a small dab from a glue stick) fabric in place (**Fig. 11**).

2. Rough cut a piece of fabric for area 2 at least ¹/₂" larger on all sides than area 2 on foundation. Place foundation right side down. Matching right sides of fabric pieces for areas 1 and 2 and having at least ¹/₄" of fabric piece for area 2 extending into area 2, pin fabric layers together (**Fig. 12**).

3. With right side of foundation facing up, sew along line between areas 1 and 2, extending sewing a few stitches beyond beginning and ending of line (**Fig. 13**).

4. Fold foundation back on stitched line, and trim seam allowance of fabrics to ¹/₄" (**Fig. 14**).

5. Open out fabric piece for area 2, press, and pin to foundation (**Fig. 15**).

6. Continue adding pieces in same manner in numerical order until foundation is covered.

7. Trim fabric and foundation along outer dashed lines to complete Unit.

8. When sewing 2 paper pieced Units together, align edges by sticking pins straight through foundations at corners and seam intersections (**Fig. 16**). Pin as usual and remove alignment pins. Stitch on seamline, extending stitches to raw edges. Carefully remove paper in seam allowance outside stitching; press seam allowances open.

PRESSING

- Use steam iron set on "Cotton" for all pressing.

- Press after sewing each seam.

- Seam allowances are almost always pressed to one side, usually toward darker fabric. However, to reduce bulk it may occasionally be necessary to press seam allowances toward the lighter fabric or even to press them open.

- To prevent dark fabric seam allowance from showing through light fabric, trim darker seam allowance slightly narrower than lighter seam allowance.

- To press long seams, such as those in long strip sets, without curving or other distortion, lay strips across width of the ironing board.

QUILTING

Quilting holds the three layers (top, batting, and backing) of the quilt together and can be done by hand or machine. Because marking, layering, and quilting are interrelated and may be done in different orders depending on circumstances, please read entire **Quilting** section, pages 55 – 59, before beginning project.

TYPES OF QUILTING DESIGNS

In the Ditch Quilting

Quilting along seamlines or along edges of appliquéd pieces is called "in the ditch" quilting. This type of quilting should be done on side **opposite** seam allowance and does not have to be marked.

Outline Quilting

Quilting a consistent distance, usually ¼", from seam or appliqué is called "outline" quilting. Outline quilting may be marked, or ¼" masking tape may be placed along seamlines for quilting guide. (Do not leave tape on quilt longer than necessary, since it may leave an adhesive residue.)

Motif Quilting

Quilting a design, such as a feathered wreath, is called "motif" quilting. This type of quilting should be marked before basting quilt layers together.

Echo Quilting

Quilting that follows the outline of an appliquéd or pieced design with two or more parallel lines is called "echo" quilting. This type of quilting does not need to be marked.

Channel Quilting

Quilting with straight, parallel lines is called "channel" quilting. This type of quilting may be marked or stitched using a guide.

Crosshatch Quilting

Quilting straight lines in a grid pattern is called "crosshatch" quilting. Lines may be stitched parallel to edges of quilt or stitched diagonally. This type of quilting may be marked or stitched using a guide.

Meandering Quilting

Quilting in random curved lines and swirls is called "meandering" quilting. Quilting lines should not cross or touch each other. This type of quilting does not need to be marked.

Stipple Quilting

Meandering quilting that is very closely spaced is called "stipple" quilting. Stippling will flatten the area quilted and is often stitched in background areas to raise appliquéd or pieced designs. This type of quilting does not need to be marked.

"*Eric sat silently and watched his son quilt. Then he moved his chair a little closer. He cleared his throat. 'You're not stitching a straight line.'*

'Anybody can do that.'

'Not your mother.'

Noah laughed a little. His eyes flicked to his father, then back down to the quilt. 'I'm following my own design. Ms. Henry says that it's okay in these squares between the stars, that she'll follow my lead in the other ones if what I do's worthwhile.'"

—from Touching Stars

Fig. 17

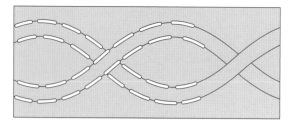

Fig. 18

Fig. 19

Fig. 20

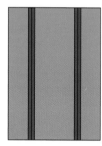

MARKING QUILTING LINES

Quilting lines may be marked using fabric marking pencils, chalk markers, or water- or air-soluble pens.

Simple quilting designs may be marked with chalk or chalk pencil after basting. A small area may be marked, then quilted, before moving to next area to be marked. Intricate designs should be marked before basting using a more durable marker.

Caution: Pressing may permanently set some marks. **Test** different markers **on scrap fabric** to find one that marks clearly and can be thoroughly removed.

A wide variety of pre-cut quilting stencils, as well as entire books of quilting patterns, are available. Using a stencil makes it easier to mark intricate or repetitive designs.

To make a stencil from a pattern, center template plastic over pattern and use a permanent marker to trace pattern onto plastic. Use a craft knife with single or double blade to cut channels along traced lines (**Fig. 17**).

PREPARING THE BACKING

To allow for slight shifting of quilt top during quilting, backing should be approximately 4" larger on all sides. Yardage requirements listed for quilt backings are calculated for 43"/44"w fabric. Using 90"w or 108"w fabric for the backing of a bed-sized quilt may eliminate piecing. To piece a backing using 43"/44"w fabric, use the following instructions.

1. Measure length and width of quilt top; add 8" to each measurement.

2. If determined width is 79" or less, cut backing fabric into two lengths slightly longer than determined *length* measurement. Trim selvages. Place lengths with right sides facing and sew long edges together, forming tube (**Fig. 18**). Match seams and press along one fold (**Fig. 19**). Cut along pressed fold to form single piece (**Fig. 20**).

3. If determined width is more than 79", it may require less fabric yardage if the backing is pieced horizontally. Divide determined *length* measurement by 40" to determine how many widths will be needed. Cut required number of widths the determined *width* measurement. Trim selvages. Sew long edges together to form single piece.

4. Trim backing to size determined in Step 1; press seam allowances open.

CHOOSING THE BATTING

The appropriate batting will make quilting easier. For fine hand quilting, choose low-loft batting. All cotton or cotton/polyester blend battings work well for machine quilting because the cotton helps "grip" quilt layers. If quilt is to be tied, a high-loft batting, sometimes called extra-loft or fat batting, may be used to make quilt "fluffy."

Types of batting include cotton, polyester, cotton/polyester blend, wool, cotton/wool blend, and silk.

When selecting batting, refer to package labels for characteristics and care instructions. Cut batting same size as prepared backing.

ASSEMBLING THE QUILT

1. Examine wrong side of quilt top closely; trim any seam allowances and clip any threads that may show through front of the quilt. Press quilt top, being careful not to "set" any marked quilting lines.

2. Place backing *wrong* side up on flat surface. Use masking tape to tape edges of backing to surface. Place batting on top of backing fabric. Smooth batting gently, being careful not to stretch or tear. Center quilt top *right* side up on batting.

3. If hand quilting, begin in center and work toward outer edges to hand baste all layers together. Use long stitches and place basting lines approximately 4" apart (**Fig. 21**). Smooth fullness or wrinkles toward outer edges.

4. If machine quilting, use 1" rustproof safety pins to "pin-baste" all layers together, spacing pins approximately 4" apart. Begin at center and work toward outer edges to secure all layers. If possible, place pins away from areas that will be quilted, although pins may be removed as needed when quilting.

Fig. 21

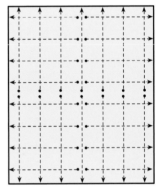

HAND QUILTING

The quilting stitch is a basic running stitch that forms a broken line on quilt top and backing. Stitches on quilt top and backing should be straight and equal in length.

1. Secure center of quilt in hoop or frame. Check quilt top and backing to make sure they are smooth. To help prevent puckers, always begin quilting in the center of quilt and work toward outside edges.

2. Thread needle with 18" - 20" length of quilting thread; knot one end. Using thimble, insert needle into quilt top and batting approximately $1/2$" from quilting line. Bring needle up on quilting line (**Fig. 22**); when knot catches on quilt top, give thread a quick, short pull to "pop" knot through fabric into batting (**Fig. 23**).

Fig. 22

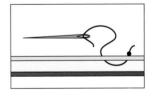

Fig. 23

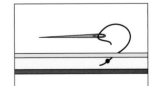

Fig. 24

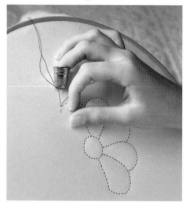

"'Now you and Noah take a good look at what I'm doing.' Helen poked the needle straight down through the quilt layers, using the thimble on her middle finger. 'See, my other hand's just underneath, and the minute I feel the tiniest prick I bring the tip up like this until I can feel it with my top thumb, then repeat. See how little fabric each stitch covers? See how the needle rocks?'"

—from Touching Stars

3. Holding needle with sewing hand and placing other hand underneath quilt, use thimble to push tip of needle down through all layers. As soon as needle touches finger underneath, use that finger to push tip of needle only back up through layers to top of quilt. (The amount of needle showing above fabric determines length of quilting stitch.) Referring to **Fig. 24**, rock needle up and down, taking three to six stitches before bringing needle and thread completely through layers. Check back of quilt to make sure stitches are going through all layers. If necessary, make one stitch at a time when quilting through seam allowances or along curves and corners.

4. At end of thread, knot thread close to fabric and "pop" knot into batting; clip thread close to fabric.

5. Move hoop as often as necessary. Thread may be left dangling and picked up again after returning to that part of quilt.

MACHINE QUILTING METHODS

Use general-purpose thread in bobbin. Do not use quilting thread. Thread the needle of machine with general-purpose thread or transparent monofilament thread to make quilting blend with quilt top fabrics. Use decorative thread, such as a metallic or contrasting-color general-purpose thread, to make quilting lines stand out more.

Straight-Line Quilting

The term "straight-line" is somewhat deceptive, since curves (especially gentle ones) as well as straight lines can be stitched with this technique.

1. Set stitch length for six to ten stitches per inch and attach walking foot to sewing machine.

2. Determine which section of quilt will have longest continuous quilting line, oftentimes area from center top to center bottom. Roll up and secure each edge of quilt to help reduce the bulk, keeping fabrics smooth. Smaller projects may not need to be rolled.

3. Begin stitching on longest quilting line, using very short stitches for the first $1/4$" to "lock" quilting. Stitch across project, using one hand on each side of walking foot to slightly spread fabric and to guide fabric through machine. Lock stitches at end of quilting line.

4. Continue machine quilting, stitching longer quilting lines first to stabilize quilt before moving on to other areas.

Free-Motion Quilting

Free-motion quilting may be free form or may follow a marked pattern.

1. Attach darning foot to sewing machine and lower or cover feed dogs.

2. Position quilt under darning foot; lower foot. Holding top thread, take a stitch and pull bobbin thread to top of quilt. To "lock" beginning of quilting line, hold top and bobbin threads while making three to five stitches in place.

3. Use one hand on each side of darning foot to slightly spread fabric and to move fabric through the machine. Even stitch length is achieved by using smooth, flowing hand motion and steady machine speed. Slow machine speed and fast hand movement will create long stitches. Fast machine speed and slow hand movement will create short stitches. Move quilt sideways, back and forth, in a circular motion, or in a random motion to create desired designs; do not rotate quilt. Lock stitches at end of each quilting line.

MAKING A HANGING SLEEVE

Attaching a hanging sleeve to back of wall hanging or quilt before the binding is added allows project to be displayed on wall.

1. Measure width of quilt top edge and subtract 1". Cut piece of fabric 7"w by determined measurement.

2. Press short edges of fabric piece $1/4$" to wrong side; press edges $1/4$" to wrong side again and machine stitch in place.

3. Matching wrong sides, fold piece in half lengthwise to form tube.

4. Follow project instructions to sew binding to quilt top and to trim backing and batting. Before Blindstitching binding to backing, match raw edges and stitch hanging sleeve to center top edge on back of quilt.

5. Finish binding quilt, treating hanging sleeve as part of backing.

6. Blindstitch bottom of hanging sleeve to backing, taking care not to stitch through to front of quilt.

7. Insert dowel or slat into hanging sleeve.

BINDING

Binding encloses the raw edges of quilt. Because of its stretchiness, bias binding works well for binding projects with curves or rounded corners and tends to lie smooth and flat in any given circumstance. Binding may also be cut from straight lengthwise or crosswise grain of fabric.

MAKING CONTINUOUS BIAS BINDING

Bias strips for binding can simply be cut and pieced to desired length. However, when a long length of binding is needed, the "continuous" method is quick and accurate.

1. Cut square from binding fabric the size indicated in project instructions. Cut square in half diagonally to make two triangles.

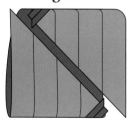

2. With right sides together and using $^1/_4$" seam allowance, sew triangles together (**Fig. 25**); press seam allowances open.

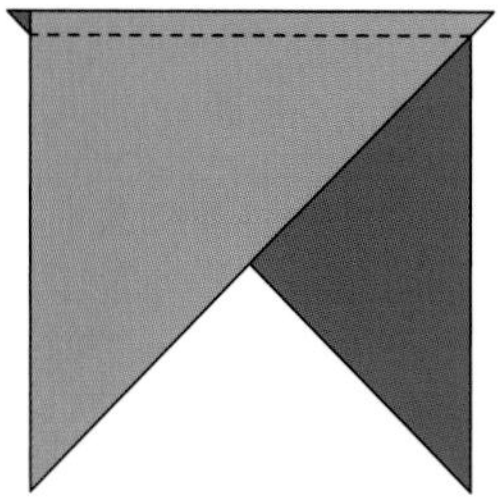

3. On wrong side of fabric, draw lines the width of binding as specified in project instructions, such as $2^1/_8$" (**Fig. 26**). Cut off any remaining fabric less than this width.

4. With right sides inside, bring short edges together to form tube; match raw edges so that first drawn line of top section meets second drawn line of bottom section (**Fig. 27**).

5. Carefully pin edges together by inserting pins through drawn lines at point where drawn lines intersect, making sure pins go through intersections on both sides. Using $^1/_4$" seam allowance, sew edges together; press seam allowances open.

6. To cut continuous strip, begin cutting along first drawn line (**Fig. 28**). Continue cutting along drawn line around tube.

7. Trim ends of bias strip square.

8. Matching wrong sides and raw edges, carefully press bias strip in half lengthwise to complete binding.

ATTACHING BINDING TO SCALLOPED EDGES

1. Press 1 end of binding diagonally (**Fig. 29**).

2. Beginning with pressed end of binding, match raw edges of binding to raw edge of quilt top. Use $^1/_4$" seam allowance to sew binding to quilt. To sew around scallops, pin binding to one scallop at a time as you sew. Gently ease binding around outer curves, being careful not to stretch it. At inner points between scallops, raise presser foot to turn the corner, keeping the fabric as smooth as possible.

Fig. 25

Fig. 26

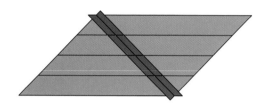

Fig. 27

Fig. 28

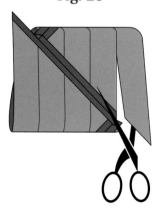

Fig. 29

3. Continue sewing binding to quilt until binding overlaps beginning end by approximately 2". Trim excess binding.

4. Fold binding over to quilt backing and pin folded edge in place covering stitching line.

5. Blindstitch (page 63) binding to backing, taking care not to stitch through to front of quilt.

ATTACHING BINDING WITH MITERED CORNERS

1. Beginning with one end near center on bottom edge of quilt, lay binding around quilt to make sure that seams in binding will not end up at a corner. Adjust placement if necessary. Matching raw edges of binding to raw edge of quilt top, pin binding to right side of quilt along one edge.

2. When you reach first corner, mark ¹/₄" from corner of quilt top (**Fig. 30**).

3. Beginning approximately 10" from end of binding (6" for *Seven Sisters Framed Block* or *Slanted Diamonds Potholder*) and using ¹/₄" seam allowance, sew binding to quilt, backstitching at beginning of stitching and at mark (**Fig. 31**). Lift needle out of fabric and clip thread.

4. Fold binding as shown in **Figs. 32 – 33** and pin binding to adjacent side, matching raw edges. When you've reached the next corner, mark ¹/₄" from edge of quilt top.

5. Backstitching at edge of quilt top, sew pinned binding to quilt (**Fig. 34**); backstitch at the next mark. Lift needle out of fabric and clip thread.

6. Continue sewing binding to quilt, stopping approximately 10" from starting point (4" for *Seven Sisters Framed Block* or *Slanted Diamonds Potholder*) (**Fig. 35**).

Fig. 30

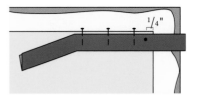

Fig. 31

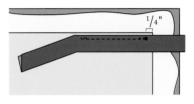

Fig. 32

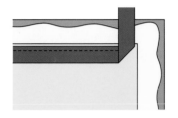

Fig. 33

Fig. 34

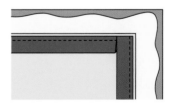

Fig. 35

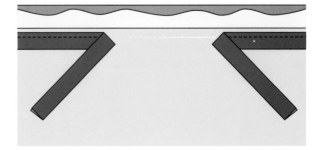

Fig. 36

Fig. 37

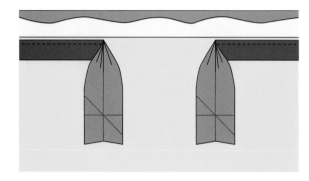

Fig. 38

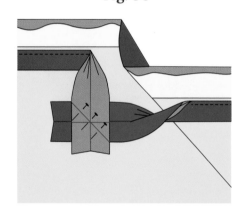

Fig. 39

Fig. 40   **Fig. 41**

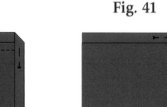

7. Bring beginning and end of binding to center of opening and fold each end back, leaving a ¹/₄" space between folds (**Fig. 36**). Finger press folds.

8. Unfold ends of binding and draw a line across wrong side in finger-pressed crease. Draw a line through the lengthwise pressed fold of binding at the same spot to create a cross mark. With edge of ruler at cross mark, line up 45° angle marking on ruler with one long side of binding. Draw a diagonal line from edge to edge. Repeat on remaining end, making sure that the two diagonal lines are angled the same way (**Fig. 37**).

9. Matching right sides and diagonal lines, pin binding ends together a right angles (**Fig. 38**).

10. Machine stitch along diagonal line (**Fig. 39**), removing pins as you stitch.

11. Lay binding against quilt to double check that it is correct length.

12. Trim binding ends, leaving ¹/₄" seam allowance; press seam open. Stitch binding to quilt.

13. Trim backing and batting even with edges of quilt top.

14. On one edge of quilt, fold binding over to quilt backing and pin pressed edge in place, covering stitching line (**Fig. 40**). On adjacent side, fold binding over, forming a mitered corner (**Fig. 41**). Repeat to pin remainder of binding in place.

15. Blindstitch (page 63) binding to backing, taking care not to stitch through to front of quilt.